FAQ's
FRONT OFFICE

FAQ's
FRONT OFFICE

Dr. Sanjeev Kumar Saxena

AMAN PUBLICATIONS
NEW DELHI

Published By
Rajiv Jain (Aman Publications) for the Hospitality Press
LG-4A, Ganpati Bhawan,
4675-B/21, Ansari Road,
Darya Ganj, Delhi-110002
E-Mail: sshjbs@yahoo.com

Reprint 2020
FAQ's Front office
ISBN–978-81-8204-105-9

Sole Distributor:
JINDAL BOOK SERVICES
LG-4A, Ganpati Bhawan,
4675-B/21, Ansari Road,
Darya Ganj, Delhi-110002

Typesetting By :
J.K. GRAPHICS (INDIA), # 97177-82194, 93125-57182

Printed By:
Balaji Offest, Shahdara, Delhi-32 (INDIA), # 92127-19107

Preface

In today's world, hotel industry is the most valuable & expanding industry. The ingress in this industry is very discerning. To become a part of this industry, students have to face interview panel & their tough questions. Most of the eligible candidates fail to crack the interview One of the main reason for this failure may be non availability of such kind of FAQ.

It gives me an immense pleasure to inform all about my unique book titled "Frequently Asked Interview Questions". This book will be a great assistance for young aspirants who are preparing & will be facing job interviews in hotel Industry.

I dedicate this book to my father late Shri Satish Chandra Saxena.

I would like to express my heartiest gratitude to the management of Jaypee Hotel & especially to Mr. Hari Sukumar, Vice President, Jaypee Palace, Agra for his guidance & encouragement to write this book.

My special thanks to my family who is always been a source of inspiration for me. Though error if any will be my own & should not tarnish the reputations of these esteemed persons.

Preface

In today's world, hotel industry is the most valuable & expanding industry. The vacancies in this industry are very fascinating. To become a part of this industry, students have to face interview panel & their tough questions. Most of the students [illegible] of the main reason for this failure may be non availability of such kind of FAQ.

It gives me an immense pleasure to inform all about my upcoming book titled "Frequently Asked Interview Questions". This book will be a great assistance for young aspirants who are preparing & will be facing job interviews in hotel industry.

I dedicate this book to my father late Shri Satish Chandra Saxena.

I would like to express my heartiest gratitude to the management of Jaypee Hotel & especially to Mr. Hari Sukumar, Vice President, Jaypee Palace, Agra for his guidance & encouragement to write this book.

My special thanks to my family who is always been a source of inspiration for me. Though error if any will be my own & should not tarnish the reputations of these esteemed persons.

Acknowledgement

I take this opportunity to congratulate Dr. Sanjeev Kumar Saxena for his work titled "Frequently Asked Interview Question- Front Office" which is the result of his vast experience in the hotel operations as well as Learning & development. The volume is a comprehensive compendium full of reading and informative value. Chapters provide an insight of Front Office in hotel establishment of high repute. It gives me great pleasure to introduce the volume as a very useful tool both for those in the hospitality industry and hospitality students pursuing education for the profession.

Mr. R.K. Saxena
Ex. Principal IHM Lucknow & Mumbai.

Contents

A. Technical Interview Questions

Q1. What is the Front Office?

The front office or the Reception is the show window of the hotel and is the department responsible for the sale of hotel rooms through systematic reservations of hotel rooms, followed by registration and assigning the rooms to the guest.

As the front office is the front of the organization, its personnel and staff is under constant observation by guests and visitors. It ensures that the guest arriving at the hotel are received, luggage handled and the formalities of check-in completed.

A warm welcome, a smile, courtesy and genuine politeness contributes to a guest's satisfaction. As the front office is the first department that meets the guest, the first impression it creates is a lasting one and is the most crucial.

All services and facilities available in the rooms as well as in the hotel are explained to the guests by the front office.

The front office is also responsible for communication and for maintaining records of the guests who have stayed in the hotel.

The department is headed by a Front Office Manager/ Room Division Manager.

Q2. What are the attributes required to be a good front office personnel?

Following attributes are required to be a good Front Office personnel:-

1) A high sense of personal grooming:-Uniforms must be clean and pressed. Hair should be groomed well. Ladies should have their hair tied in a bun. Nails should be manicured. Jewellery and ornaments worn should be at the minimum. In short FO staff should be seen at their best at all times.
2) Personal hygiene is a must as FO personnel are constantly exposed to hotel guests.
3) FO staff should possess self-confidence as they meet many different people from many different cultures. This will make them feel at ease and comfortable when dealing with guests.
4) Communication must be correct and clear.
5) Patience and calmness is necessary as the FO is the nerve centre of the hotel where a lot of pressure is generated.
6) Ability to remember names and faces as all guests have an ego and are pleased when someone recognizes him/her and addresses them by name.
7) Possessing good manners and being polite is a must.
8) Guests like to be handled by cheerful people so a

smile should always be on the face of the person at the front desk and bell desk

9) As the job in the FO requires standing for long hours, being physically fit is a must.

10) Personnel at the FO especially those at the front desk need to possess a lot of common sense and the ability to make quick decisions as many guests approach the front desk with problems and requests and the FOA has to quickly decide the best course of action which will satisfy the guest as well as keep the interests of the organization alive.

Q3. What are the different types of Hotels?

Hotels are broadly classified according to the hotel size, target markets, location, levels of service, facilities provided, ownership and affiliation etc.

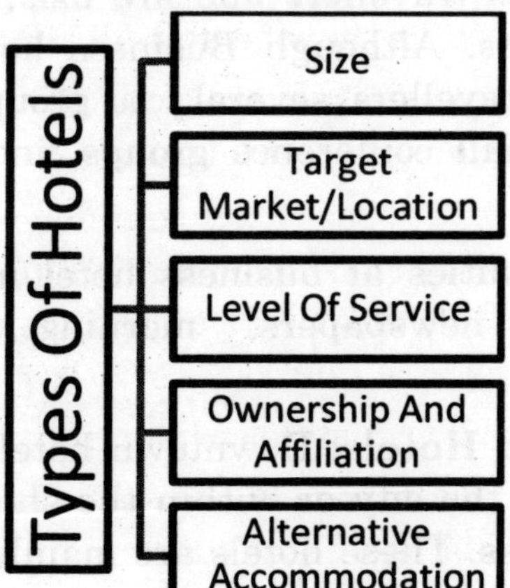

1. Size or Number of rooms

Hotels with less than 25 rooms are considered as small hotels.

Hotel with twenty six to hundred rooms are considered as medium hotels.

Hotels with 101-300 guest rooms are considered as large hotels.

Very large Hotels: Hotels over three hundred guest room are considered as very large hotels.

2. Target Market/ Location

Hotel targets several market and may be classified in line with the market they plan to attract their guests.

The common form of market includes business, airport, suites, residential, resort, timeshare, casino, convention and conference hotels.

Business or Commercial Hotels: These hotels are the largest group of hotel types and they primarily cater to business travellers and are usually located in business districts. Although Business hotel primarily serve business travellers, several tour groups, individual tourists and small conference groups find these hotel attractive.

Guest amenities at business hotel might include complimentary newspapers, morning tea/ coffee, breakfast etc.

Downtown Hotels: Downtown hotels are located in the centre of the city or within the shorter distance from the business. These hotels are mainly used by the business clientele as they find it closer to their business activities.

Airport Hotels: These forms of hotels generally target business clientele, airline passengers with overnight travel layovers or off flights and airline crews or employees. Some hotels would possibly provide free transport between hotel and airport. Some airport hotels additionally charge the guest by the hour rather than normal daily night charges.

Suite Hotels: These kinds of hotels are the most recent trend and therefore the fastest growing segments of the hotel trade. Such hotels have a living room and a separate bedroom. Professionals like accountants, lawyers, businessmen and executives find suite hotels particularly attractive as they can work and also entertain in an area beside the bedroom.

Resort Hotels: Resort hotels are typically situated within the mountains, on an island, or in some other exotic locations away from cities.

These hotels have recreational facilities, scenery, golf, tennis, sailing and swimming. Resort hotels offer pleasant and unforgettable guest experiences that encourage guest to revisit the resort.

Bed and Breakfast / Home stays: A bed and breakfast (typically shortened to B&B or BnB) is a small lodging establishment that offers overnight accommodation and breakfast. Bed and breakfast are often private family homes and typically have 1 to 10 guest rooms. They are also known as 'Home Stay's. The owner of the B&B usually stays in the premises.

Timeshare / Vacation Rental: Another new kind or segment of the hospitality business is the timeshare hotels. These are generally stated as " Vacation-interval" hotels. In timeshare hotels guests purchase the ownership of accommodations for a specific period. These owners may also have the unit rented out by the management company that operates the hotel.

Condominium Hotels: These are quite the same as time share. These units are developed on joint ownership basis. Each owner purchases and has full right of the unit he has purchased and shares the cost common to the complex, such as taxes, insurance, maintenance and upkeep of public areas including swimming pool, health club, parking, security, air conditioning, heating, cable, broad band etc. Each owner can occupy or sell his unit independently but is required to follow the rules and regulations laid by the management.

Casino Hotels: Hotels with gambling facilities are known as Casino Hotels. Although the food and beverage operations within the casino are luxurious, their functions are secondary and supportive of casino operations.

Conference and Convention Centres: These forms of hotels specialize in meeting and conferences and overnight accommodation for meeting attendees.

They also provide video conferencing facility, audiovisual equipment, business services, flexible seating arrangements, flipchart etc. These hotels mostly situated outside the metropolitan areas and have facilities like golf, swimming pool, tennis court, fitness centre, spa etc.

Transient Hotels: Mostly occupied by the travellers as a stopover of their journey. These hotels are located near the airport, railway station, sea port.

Boutique Hotels: A boutique hotels is the reverse of the standard cookie-cutter hotel. The "boutique" aspect offers guests a vacation setting with original decor or services.

Perhaps the architecture is notable or the hotel has period furniture, artistic touches or other fetching themes.

Suburban Hotels: As the name signifies that these types of hotels are located in the suburbs. It has the advantage of quieter surrounding. Rates quoted are moderate to low. Such hotels are ideal for budget traveller.

Serviced apartments: Serviced Apartment/ Residential hotels offer long-term or permanent accommodation for guest. Usually guest makes a lease agreement with the hotel for the minimum of 1 month up to a year.

Rooms usually include living room, bedroom, kitchen, private balcony, washing machines, kitchen utensils etc. Unlike traditional hotels serviced apartment only offer weekly one housekeeping service.

Heritage Hotels: Heritage hotels are those properties which originally were the forts, mansions and palaces of the erstwhile royal families of India. They were built by the royalty or their nobility in the form of their residences. These houses from centuries, have been known for their flawless royal hospitality. Today, while some of the heritage hotels are handled by the royal family themselves, others have been given to major hotels chains on lease who have now become the present-day caretakers.

Motel: A motel is a hotel designed for motorists and usually has a parking area for motor vehicles It is a type of hotel consisting of a single building of connected rooms whose door faced a parking lot and in some circumstances, a common area or a series of small cabins with common parking.

Floatel: The hotels which float on water are called floatel. The best examples of floatel in India are House boats of the dal lake of Kashmir. These are luxurious suites consisting of drawing room, dining room, bed room, sitting room, balcony, kitchen, bathroom etc. These days luxury ships are becoming popular for travelling. The guests are offered cabins to stay. These hotels float on sea water and have all the facilities of a five star hotels.

Rotel: The hotels which rotate on wheels are called Rotel. It is also called motel on wheels. Best example of rotel in India is "Palace on Wheels". It is a luxurious train, fully air-conditioned, and well furnished with attached restaurant and bar. The fare is inclusive of train ticket, food, alcoholic beverages and sightseeing.

3. Levels of service

World class service: These are also called luxury/ five star hotels. They target top business executives, entertainment celebrities, high- ranking political figures, and wealthy clientele as their primary market. They provide upscale restaurants and lounges, Valet, concierge services and also private dining facilities.

Mid-Range Service: Hotel offering either mid-range or 3 to 4-star hotels service appeals the largest segment of the travelling public. These kinds of hotels do not provide elaborate service and have an adequate staffing. They also provide uniformed service, food and beverage room service, in-room entertainments, Wi-Fi etc.

Budget / Limited Service: These hotels provide clean, comfortable, safe, inexpensive rooms and meet the basic need of guests. Budget hotels appeal primarily to budget-minded travellers who want a room with minimum services and amenities required for the comfortable stay, without paying unnecessary additional cost for costly services.

4. Ownership and Affiliations

Independent / Single Owner Hotel: They do not have identifiable ownership or management affiliation with other properties. Example of the same would be family owned and operated hotel that is not following any corporate policies or procedures.

Chain hotel: These hotels are part of a hotel chain and these kinds of ownership usually impose certain minimum standards, rules, policies and procedures to restrict affiliate activities. In general the more centralised the organisation the stronger the control over the individual property.

Management Contracts: It is a contract between the owner of the property and a hotel operator (management contractor) by which the owner employs the operator as an agent to assume the full responsibilities for operating and managing the hotel. The operator can be a hotel chain with reputed name and market image, such as Hilton, Sheraton, Best Western, Choice Hospitality, etc.

Franchise: It is the authorization given by a company to another company or individual to sell its unique product /services and use its trademark according to the guidelines given by former, for a specified time, and a specified place. Under it the owner operates as a member of the chain, utilizing the brand image, name, goodwill and obtaining for a certain fee. Some of the franchising companies are Holiday Inn, Choice International, Ramada, Hotels.

Referral Groups: It consists of independent hotel which have grouped together for some common purpose. Though the properties in the referral group may be different from each other but there is sufficient consistency in the quality of service to satisfy guest expectations. The member hotels recommend guest to other member hotels. Best Western International, one of the largest hotel chain, is the best example of referral groups.

5. Alternative Accommodation: 1)

Sarai/ Dharamshala: These lodging properties are mostly found at popular pilgrimage places.

Dak Bungalow/Circuit Houses/Inspection Bungalow/First lodges: A legacy of the British Raj, these were built as rest houses for colonial official across the country as well as in remote areas and scenic localities. These are owned by the various state governments and can be accessed through the local district administration.

Lodges/Boarding House: lodges are modest hotel situated away from the centre of the city or located at a remote destination. These are self-sufficient establishment that offer standard facilities, such as clean and comfortable rooms. Boarding houses are establishment that usually provide accommodation and meals at a specified period of time, such as weekends, or for a specified time of stay.

Youth Hostel: The youth from rural as well as urban areas, travel for various reasons, such as education, adventures and recreation. Youth hostels are established to cater to the youth on the move, who could not afford steep hotel tariff.

YatriNiwas: A yatriniwas provides low-cost, self-service accommodation to domestic tourist in cities.

Camping Grounds /Tourist camps: Camping grounds are normally located within cities in open spaces. They provide parking space along with water, electricity and toilets.

Railway/Airport Retiring Rooms: A retiring room is for the convenience of the transit travellers. These are situated at major railway station, domestic and international airports.

Paying Guest Accommodation: A paying guest accommodation is a non-institutional accommodation offered by individual household at various destinations. This kind of accommodation is becoming popular in large metropolitan cities among outstation students and the employed youth migrants from other towns.

Q4. Who does the classification of the hotel?

The classification is done by Ministry of Tourism under which, a committee formed which is known as HRACC (Hotels and Restaurants Approval & Classification committee)

- Chaired by Additional Director General (Tourism), Govt. of India/ Chairperson (HRACC) or a representative nominated by him
- Representative from FHRAI
- Representative from HAI
- Representative from IATO
- Representative from TAAI
- Principal Institute of Hotel Management or his/her representative who shall be the member of teaching faculty of the Institute.

- Regional Director, India tourism Office / local India tourism office
- Member Secretary HRACC • In case of Heritage category, a representative of Indian Heritage Hotels Association (IHHA)

This is a permanent committee to classify hotels into 1-5 star categories. Generally inspects ones in three years In case of 4 stars, 5 Star, 5 Star deluxe categories, the procedures is to apply on a prescribed application form to director general of tourism.

Q5. What are the facilities & services needed by the hotel to get 5*/5* deluxe classification?

Following are the facilities & services needed to get 5*/5* deluxe classification as per ministry of tourism government of India guidelines:-

FACILITIES & SERVICES	5*/ 5*D
Full time operation 7 days a week in season	N
Establishment to have all necessary trading licenses /Permissions	N
Establishment to have public liability insurance	D
24hr. lifts for buildings higher than ground plus two floors	N
Bedrooms, Bathrooms, Public areas and kitchen fully services daily	N
All floor surfaces clean and in good shape	N
Minimum 10 lettable rooms, all rooms with outside windows / ventilation.	N
Minimum size of bed room excluding bathroom in sq.ft.	200
Air – conditioning - % of Rooms	100%

A clean change of bed and bath linen daily and between check –in	N
Guest linen	
Minimum bed width for single 90 cm and double180 cm.	N
Mattress thickness minimum 10 cm	N
Full time operation 7 days a week in season	N
Minimum size of bed room excluding bathroom in sq.ft.	200
Air – conditioning - % of Rooms	100%
A clean change of bed and bath linen daily and between check –in	N
Minimum bed width for single 90 cm and double180 cm.	N
Mattress thickness minimum 10 cm	N
A 5 amp earthed power socket	N
A bedside table and drawer	N
TV Cable if available	N
A writing surface with sufficient lighting	N
Chairs	N
Waste paper basket	N
Opaque curtains or screening at all windows	N
A mirror at least half length (3ft.)	N
A stationary folder containing stationary	N
A 'do not disturb' notice	N
Night spread / bed cover	N
Energy saving lighting	N
Linen Room	N
Number of rooms with attached bathrooms	All
Minimum size of bathroom in square feet	45
1 bath towel and 1 hand towel to be provided per guest	N

Bath Mat	N
Guest toiletries to be provided. Minimum 1 new soap per guest.	N
Bottled toiletry products to be provided.	N
Clothes – hooks in each bath / shower room	N
Sanitary bin	N
Each western WC toilet to have a seat with lid and toilet paper.	N
All Star hotels shall provide water sprays or bidets or washlets or other modern	N
Water based post- toilet – paper hygiene facilities.	
Floors and walls to have non – porous surfaces	N
Hot and Cold running water available 24 hours	N
Shower cabin	N
Bath tubs	D
Water saving taps and showers	N
Energy saving lighting	N
Lounge or seating area in the lobby	N
Reception facility	N
Valet (parking) services to be available	N
Availability of Room, F&B and other tariff	N
Heating and cooling to be provided in public areas	N
Public rest rooms for ladies and gents, a wash basin with running hot and cold water, a mirror, a sanitary bin with lid in unisex & ladies toilet	N
At least one room for the differently abled guest	N
Bathroom	N
Ramps with anti-slip floors at the entrance. Minimum door width should be one meter to allow wheel chair access	N
Public Restrooms	N

FOOD & BEVERAGE OUTLETS	
5 Star category (with alcohol service or with no alcohol service) and 5 Star Deluxe	
Grade A cities:	
One 24 hour Multi Cuisine Restaurant cum Coffee Shop, one Specialty Restaurant and 24 hr. Room Service.	
The Specialty Restaurant may either be indoors with air – conditioning, or outdoor. The Specialty restaurant must serve specific form of cuisine. The Specialty restaurant may be open for lunch/ dinner	
Cities other than Grade A cities:	
One 24 hour Multi Cuisine Restaurant cum Coffee Shop and 24 hr. Room Service. One Specialty Restaurant would be desirable.	
Crockery and glassware	N
Cutlery to be at least stainless steel	N
Bar	N
Refrigerator with deep freezer	N
Segregated storage of meat, fish and vegetables	N
Tiled walls, non slip floors	N
Colour coded synthetic chopping boards	N
Head covering for production staff	N
Daily germicidal cleaning of floors	N
Good quality cooking vessels / utensils	N
All food grade equipment containers.	N
Drinking water	N
Ventilation system	N
Garbage to be segregated – wet and dry	N
Wet garbage area to be air-conditioned.	N
Receiving areas and stores distinct from garbage area.	N

Six monthly medical check ups for production staff	N
First aid training for all kitchen staff	N
Pest control	N
Staff uniforms for front of the house.	N
English speaking front office staff	N
Percentage of Supervisory Staff	80%
Percentage of skilled staff	60%
Staff Rest Rooms	N
Staff locker Rooms	N
Toilet facilities	N
Separate Dining area & Facility	N
Guest Services	
Provision for wheelchair for the differently abled guest	N
Valet (parking) services to be available	N
Dry cleaning / laundry	N
Tea / coffee making facility in the room	N
Iron and Iron Board facility	N
Paid transportation on call	N
Shoe cleaning shoe horn & Slippers	N
Ice (from drinking water) on demand	N
Acceptance of common credit cards and facility/ infrastructure for accepting/ making payments by digital transactions	N
Assistance with luggage on request	N
A public telephone on premises. Unit charges made known	N
Wake – up call service on request	N
Messages for guests to be recorded and delivered	N
Name address and telephone number of doctors with front desk	N

Stamps and mailing facilities	D
Newspapers available	N
Access to travel desk facilities	N
Left luggage facilities	N
Provision for emergency supplies toiletries / first aid kit	N
Health – Fitness and Barber's Shop	N
Beauty Salon and Barber's Shop	D
Florist	D
Utility shop / kiosk	D
Money changing facilities	D
Metal detectors (door frame or hand held)	N
CCTV at strategic location	N
X-Ray Machine	N
Under belly scanners to screen vehicles.	N
Verification	N
Staff trained in firefighting Drill	N
Security arrangements for all hotels entrances.	N
Each bedroom door to be fitted with lock and key, viewport / peephole & internal securing device.	N
Smoke Detectors	N
Fire and Emergency alarms should have visual & audible signals.	N
First aid kit with over the counter medicines at the front desk	N
Fire Exit Signs on guest floors with emergency / backup power.	N
Telephone facility within arm's reach of the toilet seat	N
Provide at least two multi – purpose sockets	N
A telephone for incoming & outgoing calls in the room	N

PC available for guest use with internet access	N
E-mail service	N
Fax, photocopy and printing Services.	N
In room Internet / wi-fi connection	N
Business Centre	N
Swimming Pool	N
Parking Facilities	N
Conference Facilities.	N
Sewage Treatment Plant	N
Rain Water Harvesting	N
Waste management	N
Pollution control mothods for air, water and light	N
Introduction of non CFC equipment for refrigeration and air conditioning and other Eco-friendly measures / initiatives.	N
D Desirable N- Necessary	

Q6. What are the different types of rooms?

In hotels, the rooms are categorised and priced according to the type of bed, number of occupants, number of bed, decor, specific furnishings or features and now days even the special themes are available in the room.

Later when assigning the guest room before the arrival of the guest the front desk agent must be aware of guest room characteristics for each room type available in the hotel. Also not to forget any guest specific request or room specific request requested by the guest for eg:- room away from the elevator, king bedded room, twin bedroom.

Following room type definitions are common in the hotel industry :

1. **Single:** A room assigned to one person. May have one or more beds and is generally sized between 37 m^2 to 45 m^2.

2. **Double:** A room assigned to two people. May have one or more beds and is generally sized between 40 m^2 to 45 m^2.
3. **Triple:** A room that can accommodate three persons and has been fitted with three twin beds, one double bed and one twin bed or two double beds and is generally sized between 45 m^2 to 65 m^2.
4. **Quad:** A room assigned to four people. May have two or more beds and is generally sized between 70 m^2 to 85 m^2.
5. **Queen:** A room with a queen-sized bed may be occupied by one or more people and is generally sized between 32 m^2 to 50 m^2.
6. **King:** A room with a king-sized bed may be occupied by one or more people and is generally sized between 32 m^2 to 50 m^2.
7. **Twin:** A room with two twin beds may be occupied by one or more people and is generally sized between 32 m^2 to 40 m^2.
8. **Hollywood Twin Room:** A room that can accommodate two persons with two twin beds joined together by a common headboard. Most of the budget hotels tend to provide many of these room settings which cater both couples and parties in two and is generally sized between 32 m^2 to 40 m^2.
9. **Double-double:** A room with two double (or perhaps queen) beds. And can accommodate two to four persons with two twins, double or queen-size beds and is generally sized between 50 m^2 to 70 m^2.
10. **Studio:** A room with a studio bed- a couch which can be converted into a bed, may also have an additional bed and is generally sized between 25 m^2 to 40 m^2.

11. **Suite / Executive Suite:** A parlour or living room connected with one or more bedrooms and is generally sized between 70 m^2 to 100 m^2.
12. **Mini Suite or Junior Suite:** A single room with a bed and sitting area. Sometimes the sleeping area is in a bedroom separate from the parlour or living room and is generally sized between 60 m^2 to 80 m^2.
13. **President Suite | Presidential Suite:** The most expensive room provided by a hotel. Usually, only one president suite is available in a hotel. A president suite always has one or more bedrooms and a living space with a strong emphasis on grand in-room decoration, high-quality amenities and supplies, and tailor-made services (e.g. personal butler during the stay) and is generally sized between 80 m^2 to 350 m^2.
14. **Apartments / Room for Extended Stay:** This room type can be found in service apartments and hotels which target for long stay guests. Open kitchens, cooking equipment, dryer, washer etc. are usually available in the room and is generally sized between 96 m^2 to 250 m^2
15. **Connecting Room:** Rooms with individual entrance doors from the outside and a connecting door between. Guests can move between rooms without going through the hallway and is generally sized between 30 m^2 to 50 m^2.
16. **Murphy Room:** A room that is fitted with a sofa bed or a Murphy bed (i.e. a bed that folds out of a wall or closet) which can be transformed to the bedroom at night and to a living room in daytime and is generally sized between 20 m^2 to 40 m^2.

17. **Accessible Room / Disabled Room:** This room type is mainly designed for disabled guests and it is required by law that hotels must provide a certain number of accessible rooms to avoid discrimination. The room size or area of Accessible Room Types is generally between 30 m^2 to 42 m^2.
18. **Cabana:** This type of room is always adjoining to the swimming pool or has a private pool attached to the room and is generally sized between 30 m^2 to 45 m^2.
19. **Adjoining Room:** Room with a common wall but no connecting door and is generally sized between 30 m^2 to 45 m^2.
20. **Adjacent Room:** Room close to each other, perhaps across the hall and is generally sized between 30 m^2 to 45 m^2.
21. **Villa:** A special form of accommodation which can be found in some resort hotels. It is a kind of stand-alone house which gives extra privacy and space to hotel guests. A fully equipped villa contains not only bedrooms and a living room but a private swimming pool, Jacuzzi and balcony and is generally sized between 100 m^2 to 150 m^2.
22. **Executive Floor/Floored Room:** A room located on the 'executive floor' which enables convenient access to the executive lounge. Besides, some hotels also provide 'female executive floors' with their rooms assigned to female guests only due to safety and security reasons and is generally sized between 32 m^2 to 50 m^2.
23. **Lania Room:** A Lanai has a veranda or roofed patio, and is often furnished and used as a living room. It generally had garden or sea beach view.

24. **Penthouse Room:** A penthouse is generally located on the topmost floor of the hotel and has an attached open terrace.

Q7. What are the different types of room rates?

Various room rates are as follows:

1. **Rack rate:** the official or advertised price of a hotel room, on which a discount is usually negotiable.
2. **Crib rate:** Crib rate applicable to children below 12 years of age and accompanying their parents.
3. **Corporate rate:** these are the special rates offered to the corporate business houses, these rates are lower than rack rates.
4. **Seasonal rate:** these are the special rates which are offered to the guests. These rates vary from high low and shoulder season.
5. **Advance purchase rate:** these rates are highly discounted rates offered to the guests for booking the room in advance.
6. **Weekend rate:** these rates are the higher rates offered to the guests due to high occupancy on weekends.
7. **Day rate:** these rate are charged to the guests for not staying overnight in the hotel.
8. **Group rate:** a rate which is offered to the group operator which is commissionable only to retail travel agent, tour operator and wholesalers, generally.
9. **Wholesale rate:** these are the heavily discounted rates offered to the wholesalers who operate a series of tours for group arriving and departing together.

10. **Volume guarantee rate:** these rate are special rates which are offered to the business houses in order to attract high volume of business.
11. **Airline or crew rates:** these rates are offered to the airline crew, depending upon the total room night on consistent and continuous basis given by the airlines over period.
12. **Introductory rate:** these rates are offered to a guest by a hotel on opening a new property in a town.
13. **Package rate:** these rates are the act of placing several products or services together in a single **package** and selling for a lower **price** than would be charged if the items were sold separately, offered to the guest.
14. **Travel agent rate:** these are the special rate offered to the travel agent for providing business to the hotel.

Q8. What are the different types of meal plans?

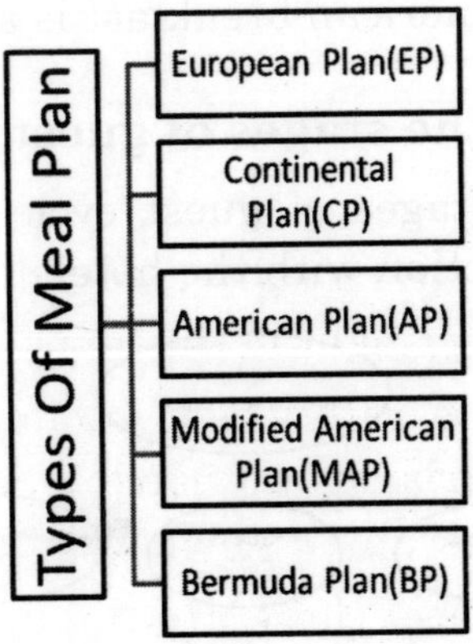

There are various meal plans which the hotel offers to the guest

1. **European Plan**: This plan is abbreviated as EP and it indicates that the quoted rate is strictly for rooms and does not include any meals. Any food & beverage provided by the hotel is billed separately.
2. **Continental Plan:** This plan is abbreviated as CP and it indicates that the quoted rate is for Room & Continental Breakfast.
3. **American Plan:** This plan is abbreviated as AP and it indicates that the quoted rate is for Room rate+Breakfast, Lunch & Dinner provided by the hotel This plan is also known as En pension (Full Board Plan).
4. **Modified American Plan:** This plan is abbreviated as MAP and it indicates that the quoted rate is for Room rate + Breakfast, Lunch or Dinner provided by the hotel. This plan is also known as demi pension (Half Board Plan).
5. **Bed & Breakfast (B&B) or Bermuda Plan:** Bed & Breakfast (B&B) or Bermuda Plan is same as continental plan but instead of continental breakfast, american breakfast is served.

Q9. What are the stages of guest cycle?

There are four stages of guest cycle where the guest makes the interaction with the hotel.

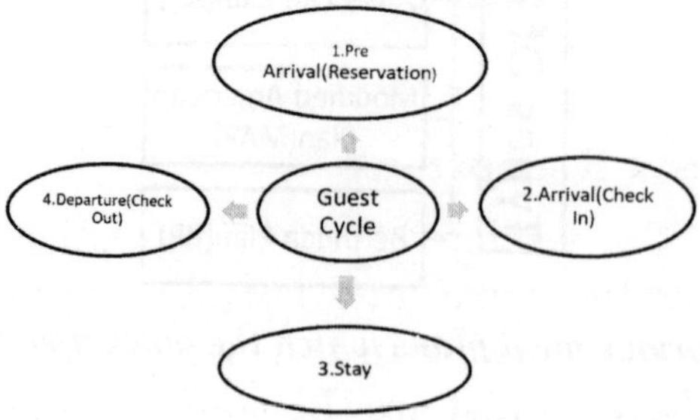

Q10. What are the different subsections of the front office department?

The different subsections of the front office department are:-

- Reservation
- Reception
- Concierge (information desk)
- Front office cashier
- Bell desk
- Telephone operator
- Business centre
- Travel desk

Q11. What is a Reservation?

Reservation is the nerve centre of the front office department. Where the guest make request for the accommodation in a hotel for any particular period. Reservationists are the employees responsible for accepting and processing of the reservation made by the guests from different modes (such as telephone, e-mail, fax, letters, CRS, personally etc), confirmation, amendment, cancelling and profiling of the guest. Ideally reservation counter situated behind the reception counter for smooth functioning. This section is headed by Reservation Manager.

Q12. What is a Reception?

Reception is the section of the front office which is responsible for the warm and friendly reception of ali the guests. Staffs working in this section are known as receptionist. Receptionist are the staff who have a direct contact with the guest, thus they should pose an amiable personality with high-level of grooming at all the times. Reception deals with daily arrival and departure of the guest, blocking of rooms for expected arrivals in advance, fill up all the necessary details in guest registration card for confirmed reservations, issues keys, facilitate the guest with the information, answering the queries and deal with complains, upselling of rooms and take reservation on phone (when the reservation is closed).They coordinate room status update with the housekeeping and engineering for any maintenance related work.

Q13. What is Concierge?

Concierge is another section under front office department, which is located at the visible part of lobby separately within the lobby area or joined together with the front desk. This section is responsible for providing information related to the hotel, room, facilities and about the city or town where the hotel is located. Concierge is also responsible for guest mails, messages, send post, arranging local monuments ticket, booking of movie & travel ticket, planning itinerary, organizing tour etc.

Q14. What is a Cashier?

Cashier is one of the most important section in the front office located at the front desk. Front office cashier, working in this section is responsible for updating guest bills, keeping up to date cash and credit transactions of the guest and get them settled before the guest departure. Front office cashier should ensure the timely collection of all guest bills from different outlets and posts them in respective folios in case if the Front Office is not computerized. Front office cashier is also responsible for encashing foreign exchange as per the regulations, disburse petty cash to hotel staff and authorized paid outs and also control safety lockers.

Q 15. What is a Bell Desk?

Bell Desk is one of the most important section in the front office, who handles the entire guest luggage during the arrival and departure. The Bell boy take the guest baggage from the car to the porch/gate, escort the guest to their rooms along with the luggage, explain the operation of light control, air conditioner, television, safety locker in room etc. He also handle guest room keys during departure, shift the guest luggage from one room to another, help in packing of guest luggage, distribute news papers, deliver guest message to their rooms, report scanty baggage guest, page the guest in public area and also get the medicine for the guest from outside the hotel.

Q16. What is a Telephone Operator?

Telephone Operator is a separate section under front office department which is located on the back side of the hotel. They are connected to the front desk and cannot be seen by the guest. A telephone operator is an employee in this section, responsible for handling all incoming/outgoing guest and hotel calls. Telephone operator is responsible for posting of all charges incurred by the guests and the hotel employees while making out calls. He also provides the wake up calls and takes the telephonic messages for the guest. He also handles any kind of emergency situations

Q17. What is a Business Centre?

Business Centre is a guest area where secretarial

assistance is offered to the guest for conducting conference, seminars, and interviews. All necessary equipment's, fax, telex, internet facility, photocopying, spiral binding, printing are available in business centre .Business centre also meet the demand for guest to translate and interpret services as well as the hire of laptops& computers.

Q18. What is a Travel Desk?

Travel desk is the section responsible for providing vehicle as per demand, organize sightseeing and book railway/air-tickets for the guest. Generally in most of the hotel it is outsourced.

Q19. What are the functions of reservation?

Following are the functions of reservation:-

1. **Taking reservations for hotel rooms**: This is the main function. They receive and process the requests for bookings from prospective guests after checking the room availability position for the required date. In case the room availability position is negative, alternate accommodation is suggested and alternate dates may be offered. They are also responsible for up selling of hotel rooms.
2. **Information:** They provides the information regarding various services and facilities offered by the hotel to the guest at the time of booking.
3. **Amendment of booking**: They do the amendment of booking, when the guest wishes to change the type, number of room and date of their booking.
4. **Cancellation of Booking**: They are responsible for releasing of rooms when the guest cancel the booking.

Q20. What are the different modes of reservation?

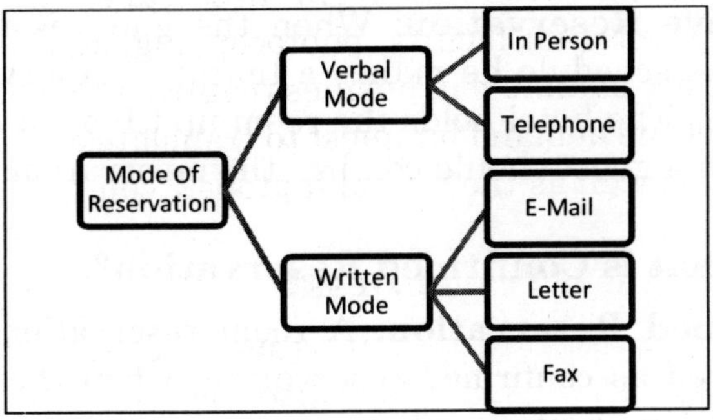

Q21. What are the different sources of reservation?

A hotel receives reservation request from different sources:

- Direct Guest
- Hotel Website
- Travel Agency
- Company
- CRS/GDS
- Tour Operator
- Government

Q22. What are the different types of reservation?

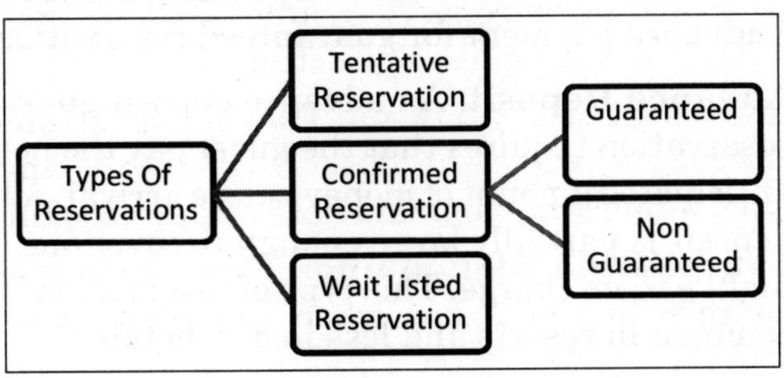

Q23. What is Tentative Reservation?

Tentative Reservation: When the guest is not sure about his schedule he makes a tentative reservation in the hotel. The hotel holds the room up till a cut off date, by which a guest should confirm the reservation.

Q24. What is Confirmed Reservation?

Confirmed Reservation: A room reservation can be considered as confirmed reservation, when the request received in writing along with advance payment. Confirmed reservation can be of two types:-.

- Guaranteed Reservation
- Non- Guaranteed Reservation

Q25. What is Guaranteed Reservation?

In the guaranteed reservation the hotel issues the guest that the required room shall be blocked after confirmation. Under this the hotel agrees to hold a room for a specific time of reservation following the scheduled day of arrival. Usually the guaranteed reservation, the advance deposit is sent through the various modes of payment for the anticipated charges for which the booking of the room has been requested. Thus, the room revenue is secured in the case of no show. The following variations in the advance payment for guaranteed reservation are:

1. **Advance Deposit**: An advance deposit guaranteed reservation requires that the guest pay the hotel the anticipated amount of money before arrival. Advance deposit is partially large enough to cover one or two night's room charge. This type of reservation is more common in resorts and less in city hotels.

2. **Pre - Payment**: This requires full payment Prior to the guest arrival. This is normally the most desirable form of a guaranteed reservation.
3. **Credit Card**: Guarantee reservations through credit card is the most popular method of payment in the business hotel.
4. **Travel Agents**: Guest pays the travel agent in advance for their tour packages and the travel agent guarantees the clients reservation. In case of no show the hotel generally bills the travel agency for payment or according to agreement.
5. **Corporate Guarantee**: This is a contractual agreement between corporation Company and hotel which states that the corporation will accept financial responsibility for any no show guest.

Q26. What is Non-Guaranteed Reservation?

Non Guaranteed reservation is a provisional reservation. In this reservation, neither there is any legal process of confirming the room nor any payment for the advance deposit made. In this room revenue is not secured.

Q 27. What is Wait Listed Reservation?

Waitlisted Reservation: Reservation is waitlisted when requested categories of room are not available for the requested dates. A waitlisted reservation is confirmed once a hotel receive any cancellation within the same class.

The hotel does not guarantee a room in case of a waitlisted reservation, it is understood that the room will be assigned to the guest in case of a cancellation or a no show. While processing the reservation, hotel informs the guest that there reservation request is on waitlist status and can be confirmed at a later date if some rooms are made available due to cancellation. This situation normally occurs during high occupancy time.

Q28. What is CRS?

CRS is known as central reservation system. It is a computerized system to store and retrieve information conduct transactions related to air travel, hotel, car rental or activities. It is originally designed and operated by airline. A CRS is the back end office system of the booking engine. It enables you to administrate rates and availabilities comfortably and easily as well as evolution of all incoming booking.

Q29. What is Global Distribution system?

Global Distribution System (GDS) is also called as Automated Reservation System (ARS). A world wide computerized reservation network. It is used as a single point of access. For reserving airline seats, hotels, rental cars, other travel related items by travel agents, online reservation sites and large corporation.

Q30. Name the premier global distribution systems?

The premier global distribution systems are amadeus, abacus, GDS sabre, galileo, world span etc.

Global Distribution System (GDS) Amadeus: It is made up of vision, values, business strategy, to support the purpose as a company. The company work with customers. Is the largest GDS provider serving the world wide travel & tourism industry. It gives access to book able content from 435 airlines.

Semi Automatic Business Research Environment (SABRE): It is used by more than 55, 000 travel agencies around the world. With more than 400 airlines, 88, 000 hotels, 24 car rental brands and 13 cruise liners. The Sabre GDS enables companies such as:- American Airlines, American Express, BCD Travel, Carlson Wagonlit Travel, Hogg Robinson Group (HRG).

Galileo: It is a part of travel port group of companies. In 2006 it has world wide market share of 22% for airline booking. The Galileo can be used to book train, cruises, car rental and hotel rooms. Travel port is a global broad based business service provider. It serves in every segment of the travel industry.

World Span: Majority of travel agents used in this system. Travel port is predominantly a global distribution system business which operates approximately 170 countries. Include internationally recognized world span & Galileo GDS platform.

Q31. What process should be followed while taking Free Individual Travellers(FIT) reservation?

a FIT- Telephonic reservation

1. Ask for caller's name / company / telephone number
2. Ask for date of reservation and no of Room, for how many nights (Single/ Double occupancy) and number of person from the caller.
3. Check & inform about the room availability
4. Describe the feature along with rate of the available rooms.
5. Determine the expected time of arrival /mode of travel.

6. Determine method of guarantee and payment as per hotel policy.
7. Any special preferences like newspaper, airport/ railway transfer, room view etc to be facilitated to guest on request.
8. Collect the E-mail Id of the guest on which confirmation to be sent.
9. Reconfirm the entire reservation detail with the guest before you close your call.

b) FIT- Fax/-Email Reservation

All such queries to be answered /reverted back within 24 hours giving detail of availability, rate, taxes applicable, check-in check out time, cut off time and confirmation.

Q32. What is a Group? What process one should follow while taking a group reservation?

A group is a body of 10 persons or more. Because it involves volume business, managements offer a special discount. The amount of discount depends on the volume of group sent and the frequency of visits organized by the tour operator. In addition to the group discounts there are special facilities with reference to hotel policy. Group reservations and correspondence assume great importance and must be dealt with quickly and accurately because:

1. Groups form a major part of business
2. The travel agent or tour operators arrangements are dependent upon confirmation of accommodation
3. Group reservation demands blocking of a large number of rooms, thus the hotel could suffer if the group is cancelled at the last minute.

4. A final confirmation of group booking takes longer to materialize charging retention is a normal practice, which may be waived by the hotel (In accordance with retention policy) depending upon:
   - The size of the group
   - Relation between the travel agent and the hotel

Q33. What are the important aspects should be kept in mind while handling the group reservation?

While handling the group reservation it is important to ensure the following:

1. The booking needs to be recorded accurately on the reservation chart
2. A separate file need to be opened for each group handled
3. Room break-up
4. Time of arrival and departure
5. Name of Tour Leader/Escort so that all matters pertaining to the group arrival may be referred to him, and to award him a complimentary room as per rules
6. Passport details (foreign guest) to complete all government formalities in advance
7. Plan of the group and rate to be charged. Payment Status if the TA is not on approved credit List
8. Any other specific instructions

The above information helps the front office to complete several formalities in advance and also to circulate the group meal information sheet to room service and restaurants.

Q34. What are the points to remember regarding reservation?

Reservation – Points to remember:-

- The reservation assistant on arrival must first check the position for the day and have the positions for the next ten days on hand
- When a guest calls on phone, the reservation assistant first checks the availability of accommodation for the day / days requested and informs the guest the availability or non-availability.
- The check-in / check out time should be mentioned and applicable tariff and tax must be quoted (while an effort is made to sell a room with a higher tariff).
- The details of the guest such as the name, address and contact information (Email, fax, and contact number), date of arrival, date of departure, flight timings, ETA (Expected time of arrival) at the hotel should be noted down .The name and contact phone number of the person making the booking must also be recorded.
- A cut off time of 1600 hrs must be given and a request should be made to the caller to confirm the reservation within that time by paying an advance or emailing a letter.
- If no advance (as per policy) or letter is received till the cut off time then the reservation should be released.
- Requests by fax, e-mail, etc. have to be replied to immediately giving details of availability, rates, taxes, check-in/check out times, cut off times and confirmations.

- Guests requiring a reservation must be informed that early check in is subject to availability.
- Guests are to be informed that if rooms are available and provided before 0800 hrs, a full day charge till 1400 hrs will be applicable.
- All reservations made though rooms are not available are to be shown as waitlisted and the same will be confirmed subject to cancellations or early departures/under stay.
- A booking can be amended by a guest by changing the date of arrival / departure (subject to policy), change in the name of person arriving or change in the number of rooms (subject to policy) required. The same is to be updated (in the system and relevant correspondence updated).
- When a request for cancellation (subject to policy) is received the same must be updated immediately so that the availability (if any) is created and a fresh booking can be taken.
- Reservations must be filed date wise for the current month and month wise for the current year.
- All reservations requests MUST be replied with a written confirmation.

Q35. What are the general practice adopted by the hotel for confirming the reservation?

a) CVGR individual room booking

The booking shall be deemed as confirmed only on receipt of advance or on receipt of hotel service voucher/ authorization.

b) *Direct individual booking by individuals*

All such bookings to be confirmed against credit/ debit card only or against advance received in cash / demand draft/NEFT.

c) *Booking made by travel agent or tour operator*

All advance bookings made by travel agents/ tour operator should be confirmed in writing. Each confirmation of such bookings should have terms and conditions specified in writing. If the Travel Agent is not on the approved credit list, payment status for the booking must be clear before check-in of the guest. The responsibility of ensuring the Payment Status is on FOM/ RDM or as per the hotel policy.

d) *Package Booking*

All package bookings should be confirmed against credit card guarantee only or against advance.

e) *Wedding residential*

Acceptance letter containing confirmation of dates, accommodation details required along with the requirement of banquet halls, with some percentage of advance (as per hotel policy).

g) *Corporate*

Acceptance letter with the confirmation of dates, accommodation and requirement of banquet hall, along with some percentage of advance (as per hotel policy) or bill to company letter stated in the conference agreement.

Q36. What does A/R/R/I/V/A/L means?

A– Acknowledge: Acknowledge the guest presence with eye contact smile by offering an appropriate hospitality greeting i.e. greeting for the day.

R– Recognize: Recognize regular guests and loyalty programme members and briefly recap the benefits being provided, i.e. upgrade or amenities.

R– Recap: Recap the reservation information and verify correctness of the guest history records.

I– Information: Information generated from the reservation and guest history (if any) to be verified and reconfirmed.

V– Verify: Verify mode of payment

A– Acquire: Acquire the room key for the guest

L– Leave: Leave a lasting impression. Warmly wish the guest a pleasant stay using the guest name.

Q37. What is Guest Registration Card?

Guest registration card is filled at the time of check in of the guest and following information is obtained from the guest:

- Name
- Address
- Telephone number
- Company affiliation
- Payment method
- Expected arrival date
- Planned departure date or length of stay
- Required room rate

- Required room type
- Room number
- Method of payment
- Special requests
- Signature

Q38. What are the accepted government approved photo IDs to be collected at the time of check -in?

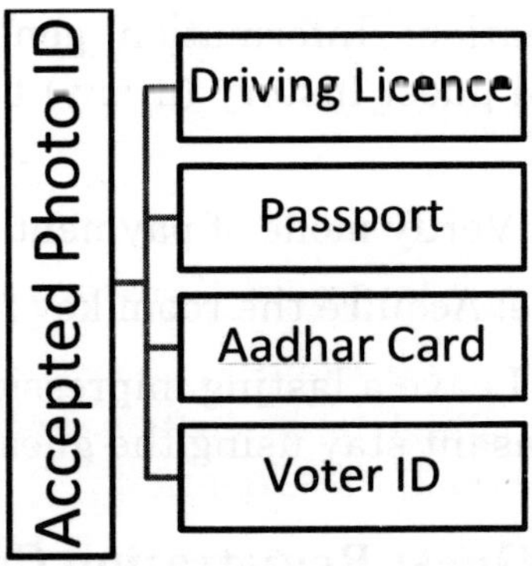

Q39 Explain the Check-in Process for the guest with confirmed reservation?

Guest with confirmed reservation

- Greet the guest. Make guest feel welcome and listen carefully.
- Ask guest name, retrieve reservation and give guest registration card.
- Request for the guest passport and business card (in case of foreign guest and check the validity of passport & visa), photo identity and business card (in case of Indian guest).

- Get the Id proof scanned or photo copied as appropriate.
- Ask the guest to complete/verify Pre-filled GRC and explain.
- Confirm details (Length of stay, Departure date)
- Depending on the availability of rooms, allocate room as per the preference of guest.
- Check registration card to ensure that all details are complete, has been signed and reconfirm the mode of payment. If cash take the advance (as per the hotel policy), if through credit card ask for the credit card details and take appropriate pre authorization based on the length of stay and billing instructions.
- Issue keys (sell hotel facilities and services/offer assistance with wake up calls and others)
- Call the bell boy to escort the guest and carry the luggage to the allocated room.
- Wish the guest an enjoyable stay and update the front office records.

Q40. Explain the Check-in Process for the walk in guest?

Registering walk-ins takes more time than registering reservation-holders.

- Greet the guest. Make guest feel welcome
- Check availability of rooms.
- If rooms are available.
- Establish the mode of settlement of bills
- Request for advance deposit.

- Confirm details (length of stay, departure date)
- Depending on the availability of rooms, allocate room as per the preference of guest.
- Issue key (sell hotel facilities and services/offer assistance with wake up calls, and others).
- Call the bell boy to escort guest and carry the luggage to allocated room.
- Wish the guest an enjoyable stay and update the Front Office records.

If rooms are not available

- Suggest alternatives/refuse accommodation politely

Q41. Explain the pre-registration activities for the group arrival?

- Prepare a group list, containing details of each guest in the group.
- Block rooms preferably on the same floor.
- Prepare rooming list.
- Arrange room keys according to the rooming list and place them in an envelope.
- Fill group registration card for group members as per the information received from the group leader.
- Arrange welcome drink for group members.
- Keep enough bell boys to handle luggage.

Q42. Explain the Group check-in process?

- Keep in touch with the group leader before the group's arrival. On the arrival, send bell boys to handle the luggage of the guests.

- Hand over the GRCs and room keys to group leader, who will get the GRCs signed by group members and distribute the keys.
- Serve the welcome drink to all group members at an appropriate place.
- Receive the signed GRCs from the group leader and check if same are complete.
- Guests proceed to their rooms and the FO circulates the Rooming list to department concerned.

Q43. What are the important points to remember during the check in?

1) Take the passport detail & business card for (foreign guest and NRI, check the validity of passport & visa) and Government approved photo Id card & business card (Indian guest)
2) If the due guest payment is more than Rs. 50, 000/- collection of the copy of pan card is mandatory (applicable for cash/cheque payment only).
3) If the guest is accompanied by husband/wife and kids (children policy will be applicable) mention the age of the kids on guest registration card (at specified space only) i.e. Adult/Child.
4) Collect photo IDs per room in case of a family.
5) If it is not a family then obtain individual Government approved photo ID from each guest staying in the room. In case of a local guest checking in, please obtain Photo Id of all the guests.
6) If the guest is having scanty baggage, collection of advance multiplied by the number of days stay, is a must. Apart from mentioning the same in billing

instructions visible to outlets (such as room service and restaurants) as well as housekeeping and security are to be intimated about the same and instructed to collect all payments directly for any food consumed or services utilized. Entry to be made in scanty baggage register.

7) In case of foreign nationals, check validity of Passport & Visa.

8) In case of Pakistan & Afghanistan nationals, check places to visit stamped in visa. Photocopy of visa application form to be obtained.

9) Room keys should be only validated for the duration of stay (time specific – in case of early or late departure).

10) Duplicate keys should be issued only after verifying the name and room number in the system.

11) Deactivated keys to be issued only after verifying the key card in key encoder.

12) No overwriting should be done on guest registration card.

13) In case of Diplomat guest, tax exemption is applicable only on service tax.

14) Travel Agent Voucher

- The voucher should be collected at check-in time. If not, collect the voucher during the stay.
- Note that the voucher should be attached with the registration cards
- Verify the details for accuracy: guest name, dates, length of stay, travel agent's name.

Q44 What precaution should be taken while taking check-in of a single lady guest?

a) Single lady guest should be treated with special care during the course of her stay at the hotel.

b) The room blocked for a single lady guest should be closer to the lobby/ elevator and no room with an inter connecting door to the adjacent room to be allocated.

c) A guest is accorded a special care status in OPERA (Open Process Engine for Reliable Activity) and to be highlighted in the briefing.

d) Operator to be informed about screening of calls. Care to be taken if someone comes to meet her or inquires about her at the front desk or on the phone. The Front office assistant / operator to call up the guest and ask whether she would like the call to be transferred to her room.

   I. A lady FOA to escort the guest

   II. The room to be serviced by preferably lady housekeeping assistant.

   III. The lady not to be disturbed after baggage has been delivered to the room.

Q45. What is arrival and departure (A&D) register?

The arrival and departure register is a formal record and control of all the arrival and departure. The main information recorded in the A&D register are:

- The date of arrival
- Name of guest
- Room no

- No of person
- Date of departure
- Name of guest
- Room no
- No of person

Q46. What is C-Form?

According to the foreigner rules 1992, it is obligatory on the part of the hotel owner to send information about foreign guest registered at the hotel. The information is sent through C Form. C Form is designed for collecting prerequisite information of foreign guest whose accommodation is made in hotel. This is indeed requirements for security point of view and it helps in identifying legal arrival of foreign guest about whom we should keep information through this facility. It's one copy must be submitted at the FRRO (foreign regional registration office) or local intelligence unit. C-Form once generated must be submitted at the FRRO (foreign regional registration office) or local intelligence unit within 24 hours. But, in case of Pakistan, Bangladesh & Chinese nationals this form must be submitted within 12 hrs. Today most of the hotels are submitting this form online.

While submitting this form, please retain in mind following things which must be filled up;

- Name of Hotel: Full Name of foreign visitor. (In block letters, surname first)
- Nationality: Number, date & place of issue of passport
- Address in India (other than tourists)

- Date of arrival in India
- Arrived From
- Whether employed in India-(Yes/No)
- Proposed duration of stay in India
- Number, Date & Office of issue of Certificate (Registration, if any)

Q47. What is departure/check out?

Departure/ Check out is the last stage of the guest cycle. It is the stage of the guest's last physical interaction with the hotel, where the guests experience the last feeling which will influence whether they choose to return or talk favorably about the hotel.

The check out process should be an efficient and organized process so that guests can check-out quickly and conveniently. This is a great opportunity to ensure that guests enjoyed their stay by asking them how everything was and asking them to fill out a comment card. Remember, as each guest leaves your hotel, you have an opportunity to create a great, final positive impression of both your hotel and your service.

Q48. What is the word D/E/P/A/R/T/U/R/E means?

- D – Deliver: Deliver a warm greeting. Acknowledge guest with an appropriate hospitality greeting.
- E- Establish: Establish a level of satisfaction. Any negative feedback to be informed immediately for corrective action and service recovery.
- P- Present: Present folio to guest as a pre- check out folio and reconfirm if the charges are correct. Explain tax structures or abbreviations used on the bill folio, indicating the total amount.

- A- Ask: Ask about settlement. Be careful towards property regulations regarding cash payments and payments through cheques.
- Company settlement or instances of credit extension to be handled carefully.
- R – Reconfirm:Re-print folio checking guest address and loyalty programme enrolment. Reconfirm with the guest and solicit signature on bill as acknowledgement of charges. Tally the final bill amount with the cash receipt or the EDC machine charge slip for credit card transactions.
- T- Thank: Thank the guest for the patronage. Check onward destination and offer reservation assistance if a chain property is available there.

  Advise international guests about airport tax and brief about the time to the airport.
- U – Usher: Use guest name at least twice during conversation and usher by lobby Manager. Maintain eye contact.
- R – Remember: Remember to offer baggage assistance and transportation assistance. Ensure bell staff reconfirms baggage before the same is loaded on to the vehicle.
- E – End: End with an invitation to return, and always bid a fond farewell.

Q49. How one should take Check out /departure from the hotel?

- A guest who requires checking out intimates the front desk by phone or comes down to the front desk and asks for his bill. FOA should enquire for bell services and confirm number of bags and if the guest requires any transportation.

- The FOA intimates the room service/outlets and housekeeping feeding the checkout alert in system.
- The bell boy is sent to the room to collect luggage and the room keys and FOA should check any last minute consumption from the mini bar with the guest before preparing the bill.
- Cashier should also reconfirm if the guest have cleared the mini safe.
- FOA prepares the bill after verifying the billing instructions (i.e. cash / credit card / company/ travel agent voucher (Personal CHEQUES Should NOT BE ACCEPTED) and settles the same.
- Cashier presents the bill to the guest and any general queries regarding the bill to be answered.
- Once the bill are in order as per the guest a receipt for cash and a charge slip in case of credit card is given to the guest along with his bill copy duly signed by him and the cashier in an envelope. (while the guest bill is being processed, eye contact has to be maintained with the guest and enquiry on the guest stay should be made with the guest being requested to give his comments and feed back on a prescribed format).
- In case if guest complain of an unpleasant experience, lobby manager/FOM to be informed. If FOA is aware of unpleasant experience of guest during stay, lobby manager should meet guest – same with VIP guest checkout.
- Ask if they might need to make any future reservations.
- The guest should be thanked, wished and the

bellboy must be instructed to load the guest luggage in the guest vehicle.

- Ask guests to check their luggage.
- Seat the guest in the vehicle and give a warm farewell.
- FOA update the checkout in the PMS and also updates the front office records.

Q50. What are the important points to remember during the Check Out?

1. Personal Cheques should not be accepted in any case.
2. In case of bill to company room rate should not to be disclosed to the guest.
3. Charge slip to be duly signed in case of credit card. Take valid credit card only and check the card holder's signature. Feed in the correct card type, number, expiry date and the authorization /approval code.
4. Consumption of minibar/ or any last minute consumption to be checked with the guest before settling the bill.
5. Discounts should not be given without the approval of competent authority.
6. Signature to be verified in case of Travellers cheque. Note down the passport number of the guest on the back of the traveller's cheque.
7. All cash payments should be handled with utmost care and should be counted in front of the guest. Cash folio must be signed by the guest.
8. For each currency exchange transaction, copy of passport to be obtained.

9. Exchange rate to be updated before 11:00am on daily basis.
10. Fake currency should not be accepted
11. All paid out to be signed by the guest.
12. On cash payment above Rs. 50000/- copy of pan card should be obtained.
13. The Arrival and Departure Register is a formal record and control of all the arrivals and departures. It is to be maintained meticulously and signature of night lobby manager to be obtained on daily basis.

    The main informations recorded are:

    - Date of arrival
    - Name of guest
    - Room number
    - Number of person
    - Date of departure
14. Encashment Certificate
    a) Name and passport number should match with photocopy of the passport.
    b) Ensure that guest name/ passport no/ room no. should appear on the certificate.
    c) Check the country currency before encashment.
    d) Check the name of currency and its form e.g cash /TC.
    e) Cheque denomination of currency before going for encashment.
    f) Currency exchange should not be torn or soiled.
    g) The certificate should be signed and stamped by cashier and also signature of guest must be

obtained before handing over the encashment certificate to the guest.

h) Give one copy of encashment certificate to the guest along with the money and attach the second copy with the currency.

i) If Travellers cheque of the foreign currency is being converted, then request the guest for counter sign on the TC and match it with the guest sign on the TC which are done at the bank and his passport.

15. All supporting should be attached with the chock out folio before the shift end and should cross check all check out folio with the summary of days departure.

16. Cashier / duty manager should mention the reason for holding paymaster.

17. Travel Agent Voucher

a) The voucher should already be collected at check-in time. If not, collect the voucher during the stay.

b) Note that the voucher should be attached with the registration card at the time of check-in.

c) Verify the details for accuracy: guest name, dates, length of stay, travel agent's name.

d) After checking what is included in the voucher, only ask the guest for payment of the extras. (The separation between extra charges and fixed charges covered by the voucher should have been done during the folio preparation).

e) All extras are to be paid in full by the guest; apply corresponding "Account settlement" operation.

f) There should always be two final folios. One corresponding to the guest extras, one corresponding to the travel agent charges (includes at least room & tax charges, sometimes, breakfast, etc.).

g) Settle the charges covered by the voucher to City Ledger.

h) Attach the voucher together with the folio and drop in to the night audit box.

i) The guest should never be shown the travel agent folio.

Q51. What are the different mode of payments through which guest can settle their bill at the time of check out?

During registration, the guest indicates the method of payment he or she planned to use. Possibilities includes credit cards, debit cards, foreign exchange, cash, travellers cheques, demand draft, travel agent's voucher, bill to company, online transfers, etc. During checkout, the guest confirms the method of payment.

a. **Credit card:** A credit card or plastic money is a payment card that allows the owner to obtain goods and service on credit terms, without paying cash. Today's business and pleasure travellers usually pay with credit card. "Plastic money" has advantages for the cardholder as well as for the hotel. The cardholder is assured instant credit to satisfy debts incurred.

b. **Debit card:** is a plastic card with a magnetic strip on the reverse side that authorize direct transfer of funds from a customer's bank account to the commercial organization bank account for purchase of goods and services. The money is automatically deducted from a bank account of the cardholder to pay for the goods and services. It is also known as ATM cards which is used for withdrawing the money from the ATMs.

c. **Foreign exchange**: The tourism and hospitality industry is among the major foreign exchange earners for any Nation. All the foreign visitors in a hotel can settle their account in the currency of their country (dollar, euro, pound etc). Even if the guests have already converted their currency into Indian currency they still have to pay the room rent in foreign currency. The cashier must know the current rate of exchange details and skill to evaluate the rates. Different countries have a different restriction to hotel regarding foreign currencies. Mostly in many of the hotels, there are a lot of tourists guest than the guest of same countries and many of the tourists pay with their own country currency so it is very important for the front office cashier to handle foreign exchange carefully because we cannot upset the guests. Hotels have to take a valid license from the Reserve Bank of India to deal with foreign exchange.

d. **Cash:** It is the simplest, instant and common method of payment which is done in local currencies as well as foreign currencies by the guest. While doing the payment, the bill is presented by front office cashier to the guest and payment is done on hand through cash. When guests indicate during registration that they will pay their bills with cash or a personal cheque, the front desk agent should immediately be on the alert. Such a guest may very well charge everything during his or her stay (perhaps only one day in length) at the hotel and then exit without paying. Consequently, most hotels require cash in advance from guests who choose this method of payment, since the guest has not established any credit rating with the hotel. Now a days many hotels discourage cash transactions.

e. **Travellers cheque**: As the name suggest it a cheque which is issued by a bank to the travellers in exchange for cash. Traveller's cheque is an international accepted cheque for a sum in a specific currency that can be exchange elsewhere for local currency or goods. It is also among the most widely accepted mode of account settlement. Traveller cheque brings down the trouble of carrying a huge amount of cash, which does not seem to be safe for long distance travellers. Travellers cheque is encashed only when the cashier receives the specimen of the cheque holder signature and tallies it with the passport details. All encashed travellers cheque are sent to the local bank for payment.

f. **Demand Draft:** A demand draft is a written order from the bank for the payment of money on presentation .It is a negotiable instrument issued by the bank. The meaning of negotiable instrument is that it guarantees a certain amount of payment mentioning the name of the payee. It cannot be transferred to another person in any situation.

g. **Travel Agent Vouchers**: Tour operators and travel agencies selling package customize tour make bookings for a guest accommodation, food and beverage and other services. Mostly they receive advance payment from the travellers at the time of selling the tour package itself. The travel agency send a voucher to the service provider (hotel) with the details of the billing procedure (direct payment by the guest or bill to TA) and the services (room and meal plan) to be provided to the traveller.

h. **Bill to company:** The big business organization makes an agreement with the hotel to provide services to their staff and customer of the company. They make a deal with hotel where-by they determine the rates of different types of rooms and meal plan to be offered. The term and condition of the payment are also predetermined. The reservations are made by the company on behalf of the staff and the company guest carry a letter from their company which is called a bill to company letter, as proof of their identity. At the departure the bill should be signed by the guest. Credit section of hotel sends a letter with the bill attached, to the respective company for payment. The company may pay the bill through cheques or by online transfers.

i. Other latest modes of settlements are:
   - Real Time Gross Settlement (RTGS)
   - National Electronic Funds Transfer (NEFT)
   - Unstructured Supplementary Service Data (USSD)
   - Aadhaar Enabled Payment System (AEPS)
   - Unified Payments Interface (UPI)
   - Mobile Wallets
   - Banks Pre-paid Cards
   - Internet Banking

- Mobile Banking
- Micro ATM

Q52. What the important points to remember while settling the guest bill through Credit Card?

Handling Credit Cards

1. Check the following to establish the validity of the credit card:

   a. Whether credit card is accepted by the establishment.

   b. Compare the name and number with the cancellation bulletin circulated periodically and ascertain if the credit card is blacklisted. Check their should be no alterations on the card.

   c. Compare card holder's signature on the credit card with that on the charge record form.

   d. With the use of an imprinter, imprint the embossed credit card number mentioned on the credit card onto the charge record form in the space provided.

   e. Enter the amount that is being charged in the total column.

   f. If the total exceed the authorized limit then we must take fresh authorization immediately. If the authorization is not further given than, we must insist the guest to make payment in cash as under no circumstances, cheque is acceptable (or) any credit can be extended.

   g. When the authorization is for a limited amount, then we must put caution mark at different levels where the guest can incur any expenditure.

h. We should also not encourage or agree to the request of the guest to pay cash and recover from his credit card. One of the conditions of the credit card utilization is that the charge should be against "sales" and not against the "payment of cash".

i. Ensure that the check or bill has the guest's signature and tally the signature with that on the credit card.

j. We should send the request for authorization against the card from the collecting bank with whom we have made agreement.

k. We must make follow up with the bank on priority and ensure that authorization is received in few hours.

l. Give the guest the original copy of the charge record form and attach the other copy with the respective bill.

OFFLINE TRANSACTION ON CREDIT CARD

In case any booking is received by email with an authorization to debit the expenses to a specific master/ visa card than we must excise more care and intelligence in handling such cases.

a) Immediately send the copy of the email to your banker with whom we are transiting to get the authorization from the issuer bank. In case the credit card number mentioned is one which belongs to a person other than the person who sent the reservation, then the bank will immediately suggest you not to honour such booking

b) We must insist the person authorizing to debit his card to send a photocopy of both sides of the card so that some relevance with the name of the person who has sent the email could be establish and signature on the card can be tallied with the signature on the prescribed authorized format. Confirmation should be given only after receiving the photocopy of the card.

c) The credibility of the email coming from yahoo/ hotmail / rediff should be discounted. The emails sent through official ID of the person shows that he belongs to some group/ organization. Such emails have better credibility.

d) We should immediately send a "scanned copy" of the format to the person who has sent the email. On receiving the properly filled up form, we should send the same to the banker for authorization/approval.

e) We should request the guest to present the identity card/ passport/ visiting card/ driving licence etc before we allow him to move to the allotted room after filling the registration card. This is necessary to check the facts with the email received for the reservation.

f) We must constantly monitor the status of the guest as far as dues are concerned so that it should not exceed the authorization limit.

g) No amount should be remitted to any tour operator/ travel agents or any agency for any " off line transaction" on behalf of the guest.

h) A photocopy of the identity card/ passport/ visiting card/ driving license must be maintained in the file at least for three months from the date of transaction and also attach with the office copy of the bills.

i) Any booking made by the email for a period of less than 07 days prior to the date of check in should be examined more carefully on top priority before sending the confirmation. Where the booking is prior to more than 07 days than the complete process as stated above should be followed.

Q53. What are the important points to remember while settling the guest bill through Travel Agent Voucher?

Travel agency voucher indicates that tho guest has pre-paid to the travel agent amounts for accommodation etc. and the recovery of such amounts are made from the travel agent not from the guest.

a) Receive the travel agency voucher and see if such billing instructions are mentioned in the folio.

b) Read the voucher carefully and determine whether it has been issued from a bonafide travel agency duly recognized by the hotel, by referring to the list of bonafide agencies as issued by the accounts department.

c) See whether all the expenses / charges are covered in the voucher: if not, open and process guest folios, posting miscellaneous charges not covered in the voucher.

d) If the voucher is from a foreign travel agency, get it authorized by the lobby manager.

e) Ask the guest / group leader to sign the folio.

f) Do not give copies of signed bills.

g) Attach the voucher and the folio(s) together.

Q54. What are the important points to remember while settling the guest bill through Bill to Company?

1. For settlement of hotel bill by the company, the company letter should be received or an email from the authorised company official, from official email Id. Only companies on the hotel credit list is allowed to settle bills of their guest at the hotel by this mode.
2. Exemption of the above rule is authorized only by the GM/FOM/Sales manager of the unit.
3. In case the company is on the hotel credit list then the FOA must check on the correspondence of booking in the reservation file check for any instruction in the correspondence.
4. In case there is no information regarding the billing instruction from the company, then the FOA must request the reservation to follow up on the full bill letter from the company. The guest must also be requested, if he can get the company to send written instruction regarding his settlement at the hotel.
5. A follow up must be maintained and in case of any changes after interacting with the company, the guest must be informed immediately regarding the same. i.e. in case the company is not going to settle the full bill or a partial bill.

Q55. What is Bill on Hold?

As the name states bill on hold indicates the bill not yet settled, the reason being numerous. Factors such as skipper, bill to company letter not received, dispute for hotel expenses etc in such cases bill has to be transferred to bill in hold mode with the approval of GM /FOM.

Q56. What is Visitor Paid Out (VPO)?

A guest may sometimes request services which the hotel does not provide. In these situation the hotel will often employ the services of an outside organization like, payment for taxi, travel agency services, porter charges, florist charges, postage and courier charges, emergency medical expenses and pay on behalf of the guest is called Visitor Paid Out. These charges are debited in the guest folio.

Q57. What is an allowance?

An allowance is a type of credit posting which is given to a guest during their stay, or sometimes on their departure, and can be either for an over-charge or as a form of compensation. The amount is deducted from the guest bill is called allowance.

Q58. What are the sundry guest services offered by the front office?

The Sundry services may include:

Messages & Paging, telephone, guest request met by the porter, left luggage handling, wakeup call handling, foreign currency exchange and safe deposit locker & security etc.

Q59. What is night auditing?

The night auditing is done by night auditor who compiles and audit all revenue transaction and reconcile the revenue statements of the outlets with a view to prepare a daily report of the day's business.

Q60. What are the tasks performed by the night auditor?

Night auditing is done during the night shift. The Night auditor is required to do the following tasks:

- Reconcile all revenue statements from the outlets.
- Post any outstanding charges.
- Balance and verify all accounting transactions, including room charges and taxes.
- Verify and validate front office cashier's vouchers/ forms.
- Detect and correct any accounting errors.
- Transfer the unpaid guest account to the city ledger.
- Monitoring the house limit of the guest.
- Prepares a high balance report of guest accounts that are near or have crossed the house limit.
- Check the position for the day and note details of expected arrivals and vacant rooms.
- Check all departures bills against the settlement summary.
- Check all guest registration cards of staying guests against the occupancy statistics and verify tariffs and taxes charged for the day.
- Check the housekeepers report and verify occupancy of rooms.
- Do settlements of credit card EDC machines.
- Post accommodation charges.
- Print reports as required by the management.
- Tracks the room occupancy percentage.

Q61. What is Revenue Management?

Revenue Management (RM) is a technique based on supply and demand used to maximize revenue by lowering prices to increase sales during periods of low demand and by raising prices during the period of high demand.

Q62. What are the key performance indicators to measure the results of the hotel revenue management strategy?

Some key performance indicators to measure the results of the hotel revenue management strategy are:-

- REVPAR– Room Revenue per available Room
- TREVPAR– Total Revenue per available Room
- TREVPEC– Total Revenue per Client
- GOPPAR– Gross Operating Profit per available rooms
- REVPAM– Conference and Banqueting Revenue per available Square Meters
- REVPASH– Food & Beverage Revenue per available seats and hour (per F&B outlet)
- Public BAR Website– Best Available Rate sold through the website
- BAR Direct– Best Available Rate sold direct by phone, email, fax
- BAR Indirect Commissionable– Best Available Rate sold through commissionable online travel agencies
- BAR Indirect Net– Best Available Rate sold through net rate online travel agencies

Q63. What is market segmentation?

Market Segmentation is "Whenever a market for a product or services consists of two or more buyers, the market is capable of being segmented, that is divided into meaningful buyers group" or we can say that Market Segmentation is grouping of buyers or segmenting the market.

Q64. What are the different market segments through which hotel get the business?

- There are different market segments through which hotel gets the business:-

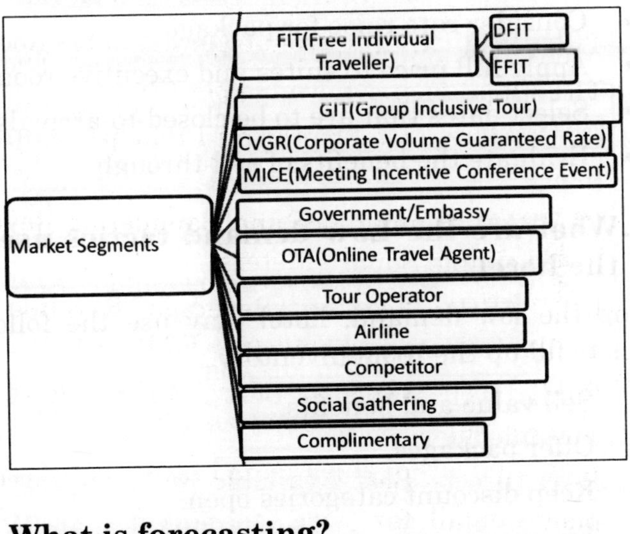

Q65. What is forecasting?

Forecasting is a systematic attempt to probe the future by inference from know facts. Business forecasting is the calculation of probable events to provide against the future. It involves a look ahead in business and idea of predetermination of events and financial implication as in the case of budgeting.

Q66. What are the high demand tactics used by the hotel?

During the high demand, hotel can use the following tactics:

- Close or restrict discounts.
- Apply minimum length of stay restrictions carefully.
- Reduce group room allocations.
- Reduce or eliminate 6 p.m. holds.
- Constrict guarantee and cancellation policies.
- Raise rates to be consistent with competitors.
- Consider rate raise for packages.
- Apply full price to suites and executive rooms.
- Select dates that are to be closed-to-arrivals.
- Evaluate the benefits of sell-through.

Q67. What are the Low demand tactics used by the hotel?

During the low demand, hotel may use the following tactics to fill up the room inventory.

- Sell value and benefits.
- Offer packages.
- Keep discount categories open.
- Encourage upgrades.
- Offer stay-sensitive price incentives.
- Remove stay restrictions.
- Establish relationships with competitors.
- Lower rates

Q68. What are the major formulas used in the Hotel Front Office?

Following are the major formulas used in the hotel front office:-

- **A**verage **R**oom **R**ate (**ARR**) = Total room revenue / *Number of rooms sold*
- **R**evpar(*Revenue per Available Room*) = Total room revenue / *Total Number of rooms Available*
- **H**ouse **C**ount = *Number of Guest staying in the hotel*
- **G**uest per **R**oom = Number of Guest/ *Number of Rooms Sold*
- **O**ccupancy **P**ercentage = Number *of room sold X100/ Total number of rooms available for sale*
- **D**ouble **O**ccupancy **P**ercentage =House count-Room Occupied X *100/ Number of Rooms Available*
- **S**ingle **O**ccupancy Percentage = *2 x (*Number of Rooms Sold) – House Count x 100/*Number of Rooms Sold*
- **R**oom **C**ount = *It is the Number of Rooms occupied on a particular night*
- **B**ed **O**ccupancy **P**ercentage = Number of Beds Sold*x 100/ Number of Beds Available for Sale*
- **O**verstay **P**ercentage = Number of Overstay *x 100 /Number of Scheduled Departure*
- **U**nderstay **P**ercentage = Understay *x 100/Stay over*
- **N**o **S**how **P**ercentage= Number of Guest did not Arrive *x 100 /Number of Confirmed Reserved Guest*

- **Cancellation Percentage** = Total Number of Cancellation X *100/Total Number of Confirmed Reservation*
- **Walk-InPercentage** = *Total Number of Walk-In in a Specific Duration x 100/Total Number of Arrival in that Specific Duration*

Situations – FRONT OFFICE

Q69. How do you handle OVERBOOKING?

The term overbooking means that there are more bookings (expected arrivals) than the number of available rooms. At this time when a guest arrives the FOA first apologises for not having a room for him citing the reason for the same (Waitlisted booking / no reconfirmation / room released after cut off time / last minute extension of stay by staying guests) and then assists the guest in making a booking in another hotel of the guests choice or if the booking has already been done inform the guest about the same. Offer to help in transferring the guest to the other hotel.

Q70. How to handle LATE CHECK OUT?

The late checkout is given to the guest only if he/she is extending his/her stay for three to four hours beyond 12 noon checkout. In case the guest is extending his stay beyond six in the evening then half day or full day charge is offered. Late checkout during sold out period is to be subjected to room availability and strictly at FOM/DM discretion. Note down all such late checkouts. While extending or refusing a late checkout the following must be considered:

1. Profile of the guest

2. Designation of the guest
3. Profile of the company
4. House positions
5. Next day's arrivals

Q71. How one can give ALLOWANCES?

Allowance entries under this classification are made to record rebates to the guest on room rate, f & b charges, telephone as per the guest entitlement due to contract or agreements as well as to rectify incorrect entries. Allowance should only be passed after taking written approval of duty manager and mentioning the reason for the same. Allowance voucher must be attached with folio.

Q72. How to handle PAID OUT?

A paid out is made only for in house guests. Each paid out voucher must be completed to indicate the name of guest, room number, purpose of the expense, date and amount. Wherever appropriate FOA must sign each paid out voucher, a receipt must be attached with the folio. If the paid out transaction is by the credit card then the guest has to be informed. Signature of the FOM/Duty Manager must be taken for any such paid out.

Q73. How one should handle WALK IN Guest?

In the hotel industry the term walk in is for a guest who enters and requires a room but has no prior reservation. If rooms are available then the FOA first enquires on the guests company name and checks for a corporate rate else the guest has to be offered rooms of a higher category and rack rates charges and the check in procedure to be followed (discount if required by the guest is only on the authorization of the front office manager / duty manager or as per company policy). It is mandatory to collect an advance payment from all walk in guests equivalent to the room tariff multiplied by the number of days the guest wants to stay plus an additional 25% for any extras or as per the hotel policy.

Q74. How to deal with SCANTY BAGGAGE guest?

A guest who checks in with little or no luggage is termed as scanty baggage and a collection of advance multiplied by the number of days stay is a must. Outlets such as room service and restaurants as well as housekeeping and security are to be intimated about the same and told to collect all payments directly for any food consumed or services utilized. In case guests is reported as scanty baggage after check–in an authorisation of the guests card is to be taken and source of booking should be verified.

Q75. How can one handle the situation of ROOM SHIFTING?

When a guest desires to shift his room to another room, the FOA gives the bellboy the keys of the room to be shifted and instructs the bellboy to shift the guest luggage and return the keys of the room that is vacated. A room move is shown in the PMS (Property Management System). Laundry and Room Service should be explicitly informed also.

Q76 . How one can handle a GUEST COMPLAINT?

A complaint by a guest must always be treated with care, as the guest who complains is one who has the interests of the organization in mind. The FOA should first apologise to the guest and then listen patiently to the guest and make notes if necessary and then intimate the concerned department about the complaint. A follow up should be done with the department concerned as to whether the complaint has been looked into. After this is done the guest should be called and feedback taken as to whether the guest is satisfied. The FOM/DM should be informed and the guest profile should be updated in brief with the problem and action taken.

Q77. How one should TAKE A MESSAGE for the GUEST?

Messages for and from guests can be given via phone or verbally and this has to be noted by the FOA and received verbally. In case the guest is physically not present in the room then the message has to be fed in PMS and slipped in the guest room though message slip.

Q78. How do one should handle WAKE UP CALLS(Telephones)?

This is a wake up alarm / reminder calls which a guest requests for. The same is noted by the FOA in a wake up call register with reminders if needed and advance orders for tea/coffee etc. The advance orders are intimated to the room service at midnight or later as and when the guests request for it and an acknowledgement taken from the room service. The FOA or the bellboy then calls up the guest at the requested time.

Q79. How to face the situation when A GUEST IS ILL?

When a guest says that he is ill and requires medical help, the FOA asks the guest whether a doctor should be called or whether the guest would like to go to a hospital. If the guest wants a doctor, the doctor on call is called to visit the guest by the FOA. If the guest wants to go to the hospital, the FOM/DM should arrange a car and visit the nearest hospital.

Q80. How to protect the GUEST PRIVACY/ SECURITY in the Hotel?

A guest staying in the hotel would not like his details given out to strangers or callers by the front desk. Visitors should never be sent to a guest room without checking with the guest first. Telephone callers should never be given details such as room numbers, names of guests, addresses etc. Guests who require all incoming calls to be screened are to be obliged. Strangers and non-residents are not allowed on guest floors without guests' permission.

Q81. How to deal with SAFE DEPOSIT FACILITY?

Safety locker is a facility provided by hotels wherein guest can keep their valuables and important documents in safety. These lockers are located in a safe place and are theft-proof. They have only one key per locker. Thus, the key would have to be kept with great care. Sometimes double custody lockers are available whereby one key is with the guest while another key is kept with the cashier or the nominee custodian of lockers. These keys are not duplicate which means that each locker has two locks. It would take both the guest key and the custodian key to open the locker. Hotels may charge a fee for the facility or give it as a free facility depending upon the number of lockers available.

Key points:

1. Ask the guest room number and tally the same with PMS
2. Before giving access to safe deposit box, safe deposit box form to be filled and signed by the guest along with his name, room number, address and signature.
3. Open the safe deposit box in front of the guest only.
4. Close SDB properly.
5. Handover the SDB key to the guest.
6. Signature of the guest to be taken every time the guest access the SDB.
7. A checkout reminder needs to be updated to remind the cashier to check about the safe deposit box keys at the time of departure.

Q82. How to handle the GUESTROOMKEYS?

Room keys are issued by the FOA at checkin. They are made for the number of nights the guest is staying. Room numbers should be written on the key docket issued at the time of check in. FOA has to ensure that keys are collected on departure.

Points to remember regarding Room Keys

1. Room keys should be only validated for the duration of stay (time specific).
2. Duplicate keys should be only issued after verifying the name and room number in the system.
3. Deactivated keys to be issued only after verifying the key card.
4. Room keys need to be collected before departure.

Q83. How to handle LOST AND FOUND?

This refers to items left back by the guest in the room or public area that is found by the FO staff or HK staff. The items found are handed over to the housekeeping supervisor/security who logs the same down in his lost and found register. Guest Profile to be updated with room number and date. If a guest enquires about the same then they are requested to identify the items lost with the security and if correct then the item is handed over to the guest and an acknowledgement taken.

Q84. How to handle DND (Do Not Disturb)ROOM?

If the room is on DND then status is mentioned in occupancy report, at 2pm floor executive will call the guest room, and in case there is no revert then slip the DND card. If found same room DND till 9 pm then Duty Manager/ HK Executive and Security Manager visits the Guest Room.

Q85. How to handle ACCIDENTS?

The house doctor is to be called immediately on phone and informed about the nature of the accident and condition of the guest. The doctor's instructions must be followed immediately. Bleeding must be stopped by swabbing wounds with cotton wool. If a fracture is suspected the guest not to be moved till the doctor arrives. This procedure is totally handled by FOM/DM.

Q86. How to handle a DRUNKEN GUEST?

Never argue with a drunken guest. He must be politely led away from public areas to an office or to his room. If he is boisterous or behaves unruly, the hotel security must be called. This procedure is totally handled by front office manager.

B. Hospitality Basics

Q87. How one should handle the telephone?

More people contact with hotel staff by telephone than any other ways. This is an unseen audience (our guest and potential guest). Ensure that they are treated with the same courtesy and consideration as our guest in the hotel. Always use a friendly tone of voice. Remember a guest in communicating over the phone is almost like communicating with a blind guest in front of you. Since he cannot see you the tone of your voice and phrases used are of utmost importance and should be clear and calm.

- Answer the phone promptly. Never let it ring more than thrice.
- Announce your department clearly e.g. Namaskar front desk (Speak slowly).
- Be ready with writing pad and pencil. For accuracy repeat back name, number, room number and message.
- Wrong way of writing the number is XXXXXXXXXX. Correct way is XXXXX-XXXXX.
- If a call is in a language not understood, be sure to call someone who does.
- While accessing information never keep the receiver open and talk to someone else. Say `May

I call you back when I obtain the information?' and be certain that you call back.

- When the call is finished, thank the guest and wait for him to disconnect and only then put the receiver down.
- Date and time all messages.
- Do not interrupt a guest who has called. While speaking do so with correct and precise words. Speak in a normal tone and accent. Do not try to speak in a different accent, as this will confuse the guest.
- Telephone lines in the hotel are for business use only. Personal calls either outgoing or incoming are to be discouraged. Emergency calls for employees will be given on the approval of the department manager.

If a guest has told you of a request or complaint and you need to transfer the call to another department or person, briefly explain the guests request or complaint so the next person doesn't ask the caller to repeat the details again.

15 Golden Rules for Telephone Handling

1. Be prompt, answer within three or four rings – callers don't like to be kept waiting.
2. Answer with a smile it comes across in your voice, making you sound friendly and positive.
3. On answering, give verbal handshake, announcing the company name and department as well as your own name.
4. Show empathy; build an instant relationship with your caller by using warm, friendly tone of voice.
5. Establish the needs of your caller immediately by asking, "how may I help you".
6. Use open questions to find out facts and information and also closed questions to clarify and check understanding.
7. If you can answer the caller's questions promptly and efficiently .if you can't help tell them what you can do for them.
8. Use continuity noises to show the caller that you are listening. For example " oh yes", "I see " or that's right".
9. Make notes, recording all necessary information. It was once said that "a short pencil is far more effective than a long memory"
10. Double-check all vital information by reading back, in summary what you have discussed.
11. Instead of passing callers around from department to department, take the callers name and telephone no. And a brief and be sure that you will pass the message.

12. Give the caller your full attention. Nobody can hold two conversations and retain 100 percent information from both.
13. Keep focused on subject in hand and do not interrupt the caller with pointless questions.
14. Remember that both people engaged in a call have the right to know whom they are talking to.
15. Sign off properly.

Winning by words on Telephone

WORDS / PHRASES TO BE USED

- Greetings
- Good Morning / Afternoon / Evening

Enquiry

- May I ask if/ for ....
- Could you please tell .... so I could help you.
- Options
- Would you prefer .... or .... ?
- Here are some options
- I suggest ....
- May I offer you ....

Apology

- I apologise for ....
- I am sorry that ....
- I am sorry to inconvenience you

Empathy

- I appreciate --------

- I understand----------
- I understand your concern

Thanks

- Thank you for ----------

WORDS / PHRASES TO AVOID

- I can't
- Its just a ----
- Policy
- Jargon
- But
- What's your problem

MAGIC WORDS

- Please
- Thank you
- I'm Sorry

Q88. What Body language should be followed during the guest interaction?

Eye contact

- Maintain eye contact with the other person
- Eyes to move between eyes, forehead and nose only.
- Do not look at lips or below the face.
- Smile as appropriate.
- Do not frown or raise eyebrows while talking or listening to the guest.

Avoid the following Mannerisms and expressions

- Biting moustache or lips, biting nails, chewing a gum or any food item.
- Scratching.
- Shrugs.
- Twitches of shoulder, neck, face.
- Fiddling with ring, watch, pen etc.

Posture

- Stand erect, shoulders back, chest out, stomach in.
- Do not stand on one leg.
- Do not lean on anything
- Do not rest hands on wall, desk etc.
- Do not put hands in pockets and do not fold hands.

Walk

- Brisk, hands not to swing too far
- Do not overtake guests walking ahead of you. If you need to, excuse yourself.

Sitting

- Erect, not slouching, ankles crossed and feet resting on the ground
- No shaking of legs
- Do not sit down in guest areas

Q 89. What Elevator etiquette should be followed during the guest interaction?

In case if there is a guest waiting with you, go first into the elevator, hold it for him to enter. Then check which floor he wants to go and press the button for him. When he has to exit from the elevator, hold the door till he exits.

Q90. What are the grooming standards one should follow in the hotel?

Grooming Standard for Females:-

a) Hair

- Hair should be neat, well styled and appear professional.
- Hair, which is of shoulder length, should be neatly pinned to keep away from the face.
- Shoulder length hair should be trimmed regularly.
- No coloured bands or metallic clips to be used.
- Hair should be neatly combed and in place at all the time.
- Hair should be clean and free of oil, should be non-greasy, and free from dandruff.
- Streaking of hair and using hair gel is permitted as long as they look classy.
- Pony tails, French braids should not exceed 9 inches in length.
- Hairs longer than shoulder length should be of even length, straight and tied up at the centre of the nape.
- The bun must be secured at the back of the head or above the nape with a black net.

b) *Nails*

- Nails should be neatly cut, shaped and clean.
- Excessively long nails are not allowed.
- Light and neutral colours of nail polish are allowed only.
- When applied, nail polish should cover the entire nail with no gaps or chips visible.
- Nails should not be chewed.
- Toe nails should be cut short and maintained clean.

c) *Jewellery*

- Jewellery on hands should be conservative and elegant.
- Only two rings are permitted, one on each hand.
- Rings should be sober and conservative and not too large.
- Watches should not be flashy or too large and should be conservative.
- Leather straps should either be black, brown or tan; metallic straps should be gold or silver.
- Dangling or large size and flashy earrings are not permitted.
- Only one set of earrings is permitted.
- Two thin bangles are permitted, either of gold or silver.
- One thin chain is permitted, either gold or silver.
- Only a small nose stud is permitted.

d) *Footwear*

- Proper footwear must be worn at all times.

- Should always be well polished and in good repair.
- If shoes are open from the back, visible heels should not be cracked.
- Closed shoes and sandals of black colour are permitted.
- Flat shoes are not permitted; there should be a minimum heel of 1 1/2 inch.

e) ***Makeup***

- Make up should not be excessive and should be relevant to business environment.
- A foundation should be used to avoid an oily look.
- Simple and basic makeup is mandatory.
- Lipstick should be matte finish, sober, and should match the uniform colour.
- Eye shadow should be subtle and not excessive.
- Eyeliner should be thin, straight and applied neatly.

f) ***Uniform***

- Uniforms should be immaculate.
- Smooth, clean, without creases and stain-free.
- Stockings should be black or skin coloured and should not have ladders or holes.
- Hotel uniforms should not be worn outside the hotel.
- The only exception to wearing uniforms outside the hotel is if you are going outside the hotel for official work.
- Pens, keys and pagers when carried should not be visible.

- Name tags should be shining and prominently displayed.

g) General Hygiene

- General Hygiene should be maintained at all time.
- Perfumes and deodorants should be mild.
- Legs and hands should be waxed regularly.
- Routine hygiene should be followed to avoid body odour.
- Facial hairs to be removed or bleached as appropriate.
- Teeth should be stain-free and there should be no bad breath.
- Smokers should use a mouth freshener before coming on duty and after smoking during breaks.
- Gargle after every meal to prevent bad breath and maintain dental hygiene.
- Hands should be washed with soap after every meal and visit to the rest room.

GROOMING STANDARDS FOR MEN

a) Hair

- Hair should be conservative and well maintained.
- Hair should be short, neatly cut and should not fall on the forehead or touch the ears.
- Hair at the back of the neck should be clean cut and should not fall on the collar.
- Hair should be neatly combed and non-oily.
- Moustaches must be neatly trimmed and should not cover the upper lip.

- Beards are only permitted as part of religious sentiments and must be suitably maintained.
- Turbans must be black.

b) Nails

- Nails should be trimmed and well maintained.
- Fingernails should be clean and dirt free.
- There should be no nicotine; carbon or ink stains on the fingers.

c) Ornaments

- Ornaments on the hand and wrist.
- Only one simple ring to be worn on either the left or the right hand.
- No bracelets or bands allowed except for religious reasons.
- Bracelets or bands that are worn should not be visible.
- Watch leather straps should be black, brown or tan and should be in good condition. Gold or silver metallic straps are also permitted.

d) Foot Wear

- Foot wear must be well maintained.
- Uniform shoes, if given, are to be worn.
- Shoes should be black.
- Shoes should be well polished and in good repair- no creaking sound.
- Socks should match the colour of the shoes.
- Socks should be odourless, clean and the elastic should be intact.

e) *Uniform*

- Uniforms must be immaculate.
- Cuffs and collars should be clean and stain free.
- Name badges should be shining and prominently displayed.
- Uniforms should be spotless with no stains.
- Uniforms should be well ironed without unnecessary creases.
- There should be no loose threads, broken buttons or any tears.
- All garments should appear fresh and not faded.
- The uniform must have a perfect fit to the individual.
- Full sleeve shirts should not be folded back.
- Belt should be plain black or brown with simple non-flashy buckle, should not be cracked or dull.
- Belt should not be more than 1.5 inches wide.
- A dark clean, small comb should be carried in the pocket.
- Handkerchief should be plain, white, crisp and clean.
- A vest should always be worn.
- Pens and keys when carried should not be visible.
- Spectacles for males should fit the face properly and should not be ornate or flashy.
- Hotel uniforms should not be worn outside the hotel while going to and fro from the residence.
- The only exception to wearing uniforms outside the hotel is if you are going outside the hotel for official work.

f) *General Hygiene*

- General Hygiene should be maintained at all times.
- Perfumes and deodorants should be mild and used sparingly.
- Routine hygiene should be followed to avoid body odour.
- Hands should be washed with soap after every meal.
- Teeth should be stain-free and should not have bad breath.
- Body weight should be within the prescribed limit.
- If you are a smoker, use a mouth freshener before coming on duty.
- Gargle after every meal to prevent bad breath.

Q91. What are the Etiquette and Manner required to be a front office professional ?

The Etiquette and Manner required to be a front office professional are :

While talking with the guest

- Always smile.
- Always maintain an interested and helpful expression.
- Maintain Eye Contact,
- Maintain distance of at least 2 feet.
- Speak softly and clearly.
- Avoid unnecessary movements of hands and facial gestures.

While Standing

- Stand Erect at ease.
- Weight balanced on both feet.
- Shoulders Straight.
- Chest out/ Stomach in.
- Keep hands on the sides or behind your back.
- Do not keep hands in pockets or on the hips.
- Do not cross arms across the chest.
- Do not lean against the counter.

While Walking-PACE

- Walk at even pace in guest areas without sound of footsteps.
- *Do not run in guest area.*
- If guests are approaching, get aside and give them first right of way.
- ***If near a door, open the door for the guest to pass through.***
- Walk on the left hand side.
- *If accompanying a guest, walk on his/her right hand side and open the door of the guest.*
- Walk erect and maintain the poise.

While talking to colleagues

- Speak softly and politely.
  - *In restaurant*
  - *In corridors*
  - *At reception counter*

LANGUAGE

- Do not use slang or abusive language, with your colleagues.

ON TELEPHONE

- Be aware of your conversation on the telephone. Guests may be watching or hearing.
- *Never shout into the telephone.*
- *Do not have long conversation, when guests are waiting.*
- Do not entertain personal calls, while at work.

Q 92. What is a Complaint?

"An expression of dissatisfaction made to a hotel, related to its products or services, or the complaints-handling process itself, where a response or resolution is implicitly expected" is termed as "complaint".

Q 93. Why do guests complain?

Guest Complain because of the following reason:-

- They did not get what was promised (expectations were not met).
- Someone was rude to them (knowingly or not).
- Someone was indifferent to them (projecting a "can't do" attitude).
- No one listened to them (an opportunity lost).
- Frustrations with matters not related to the hotel (they just take them out on the next person they see).
- Confusion or a sense of being overwhelmed (the environment is new to them).

- They are defending their ego or self-esteem (they want to be in control).
- Language barriers (they don't speak or understand the language very well, causing frustration).
- They want to impress someone (ego).
- They want compensation.

How to resolve the guest complain/ complaint handling procedure?

Listen to the guest	Listen with concern. Give undivided attention. Maintain eye contact and avoid interruptions.
Stay Calm	The calmer you remain: the better chances you have to calm the guest
Apologize for the problem	Some problems obviously call for an apology. And even if you disagree with guests, apologies make them better.
Empathize	Being sorry lets guest know how **you** feel. Showing empathy tells guests you know how **they** feel. Communicate the understanding of the problem. Use the guest's name and take the complaint seriously.
Ask questions and be prepared to take notes	Learning as many details as you can about the complaint will help you determine the best solution. Taking notes, if problem is complicated saves time if some one else needs to get involved.
Offer Solutions	Tell the guest what can do, and if possible, suggest several options. Don't make promises you can't fulfill or which exceed your authority.
Act on the problem	Follow your hotel procedures and do exactly what you promised the guest. Tell the guest how long it will take to resolve the problem. Be specific , and don't underestimate the length of the time needed.
Monitor progress	If another employee or department is involved, stay in touch with them and make sure the problem gets corrected. Keep the guest informed if there are any unforeseen delays.
Follow up	If you feel it won't disturb the guest, check back to make sure that he / she is satisfied once the problem has been corrected.

C. Basic General Awareness

Q95. What are the capital, currency and primary language of the following countries?

Country	**Capital**	**Currency**	**Primary Language**
Afghanistan	Kabul	Afghani	Dari persian Pashto
Argentina	Buenos Aires	Argentina Peso	Spanish
Australia	Canberra	Australian Dollar	English
Austria	Vienna	Euro	German
Bahrain	Manama	Bahraini Dinar	Arabic
Bangladesh	Dhaka	Taka	Bangla
Belgium	Brussels	Euro	Dutch, French
Bhutan	Thimphu	Ngultrum	Dzhongkha
Brazil	Brazilia	Real	Portuguese
Bulgaria	Sofia	Lev	Bulgarian
Canada	Ottawa	Canadian Dollar	English, French
Cape Verde	Paria	Cape vardean escudo	Portuguese
Chile	Santiago	Chilean peso	Spanish
China	Beijing	Chinese yuan	Mandarin
Colombia	Bogota	Colombian peso	Spanish

Costa Rica	San jose	Colon	Spanish
Cuba	Havana	Cuban Peso	Spanish
Cyprus	Nicosia	Euro	Greek, Turkish
Denmark	Copenhagen	Danish Korane	Danish
Egypt	Cairo	Egyptian Pound	Arabic
Ethiopia	Addis Ababa	Birr	Amharic
Fiji	Suva	Fijian Dollar	English, Hindi
Finland	Helsinki	Euro	Swedish, Finnish
France	Paris	Euro	French
Germany	Berlin	Euro	German
Ghana	Accra	Ghanaian cedi	English
Greece	Athens	Euro	Greek
Hungary	Budapest	Forint	Hungarian
Iceland	Reykjavik	Icelandic krona	Icelandic
India	New Delhi	Indian Rupee	Hindi, English
Indonesia	Jakarta	Rupiah	Indonesian
Iran	Tehran	Rail	Persian
Iraq	Baghdad	Iraqi Dinar	Arabic, Kurdish
Republic of Ireland	Dublin	Euro	English, Irish
Israel	Jerusalem	Shekel	Arabic
Italy	Rome	Euro	Italian
Jamaica	Kingston	Jamaican Dollar	English
Japan	Tokyo	Yen	Japanese
Jordon	Amman	Jordanian Dinar	Arabic
Kenya	Nairobi	Kenya Shilling	English, Sesotho

North Korea	Pyongyang	North Korean won	Korean
South Korea	Seoul	South Korean won	Korean
Kuwait	Kuwait city	Kuwait dollar	Arabic, English
Malaysia	Kuala lumpur	Ringgit	Malay
Maldives	Male	Maldivian Rufiyaa	Dhivehi
Mali	Bamako	West African CFA	French
Mauritius	Port Louis	Mauritian Rupee	English
Mexico	Mexico city	Mexican Peso	Spanish
Myanmar	Nypyidaw	kyat	Burmese
Nepal	Kathmandu	Nepalese Rupee	Nepali
Netherlands	Amsterdam	Euro	Dutch
New Zealand	Wellington	New Zealand Dollar	English
Nigeria	Abuja	Naira	English
Norway	Oslo	Norwegian Krone	Norwegian
Oman	Muscat	Omani Rial	Arabic
Pakistan	Islamabad	Pakistani Rupee	Urdu, English
Panama	Panama city	Balboa	Spanish
Philippines	Manila	Philippine Peso	Filipino, English
Poland	Warsaw	Zloty	Polish
Portugal	Lisbon	Euro	Portuguese
Qatar	Doha	Qatari Riyal	Arabic
Russia	Moscow	Ruble	Russian
Saudi Arab	Riyadh	Saudi Riyal	Arabic
Seychelles	Victoria	Seychoellois Rupee	French, English

Singapore	Singapore	Singapore Dollar	English, Malay
South Africa	Cape town	Rand	Zulu, Xhosa
Spain	Madrid	Euro	Spanish
Sri Lanka	Colombo	Sri Lanka Rupee	Sinhala, Tamil
Sudan	Khartoum	Sudanese pound	Arabic, English
Sweden	Stockholm	Swedish krona	Swedish, Finnish
Switzerland	Berne	Swiss Franc	German, French
Taiwan	Taipei	New Taiwan dollar	Mandarin
Turkey	Ankara	Turkish Lira	Turkish
Uganda	Kampala	Uganda Schilling	Swahili, English
United Arab Emirates	Abu Dhabi	Dirham	Arabic
United Kingdom	London	Pound Sterling	English
United states of America	Washington D.C	United States Dollar	English, Spanish
Venezuela	Caracas	Bolivar Fuertes	Spanish
Yemen	Sanaa	Yemeni Rail	Arabic
Zambia	Lusaka	Zambian Kwacha	English
Zimbabwe	Harare	United States Dollar	English

Q96. Name any 15 international airlines?

S. No	Name of Airlines	Country of Origin
1.	Singapore Airlines	Singapore
2.	Malaysia Airlines	Malaysia
3.	Virgin America	USA

4.	Asian Airlines	South Korea
5.	Qatar Airways	Qatar
6.	All Nippon Airways	Japan
7.	Garuda Indonesia	Indonesia
8.	Silk Air	Singapore
9.	Korean Air	South Korea
10.	Air New Zealand	New Zealand
11.	Cathay Pacific	Hong Kong
12.	South African Airways	South Africa
13.	Turkish Airlines	Turkey
14.	Finnair	Finland
15.	Thai Airways	Thailand

Q97. Name the countries in following group?

A. **SAARC:** The South Asian Association for Regional Cooperation (SAARC) is the regional intergovernmental organization and geopolitical union of nations in South Asia. Its member states include Afghanistan, Bangladesh, Bhutan, India, Nepal, the Maldives, Pakistan and Sri Lanka.

B. **BRICS:** is the acronym coined for an association of five major emerging national economies: Brazil, Russia, India, China and South Africa. Originally the first four were grouped as "BRIC" (or "the BRICs"), before the induction of South Africa in 2010.

C. **G8:** The Group of Eight (G8) refers to the group of eight highly industrialized nations—France, Germany, Italy, the United Kingdom, Japan, the United States, Canada, and Russia—that hold an annual meeting to foster consensus on global issues like economic growth and crisis management, global security, energy, and terrorism.

D. **BIMSTEC:** The BIMSTEC member state Bangladesh, India, Myanmar, Sri Lanka, Thailand, Nepal and Bhutan—are among the countries dependent on the Bay of Bengal.

FRONT OFFICE TERMINOLOGY

0-call (Zero-call)	A telephone call placed with an operator's assistance.
Access Aisle	An aisle that is necessary part of an accessible parking space. It allows disabled person with a device such as a wheelchair to enter and exit vehicles and travel to the sidewalk.
Account Payable	Financial obligatory the hotel owes to private and government related agencies and vendors.
Account Receivable	Amount of money owed to the hotel by the guest.
Adjoining Rooms	Guest rooms located side by side without a common door between them.
Adhoc Group	These are one time groups and are booked through a travel agent to avail special rates
Aging of Account	Indication of the stage of payment cycle such as 10, 30, 60 days overdue.
All Inclusive	It stands for all inclusive rates ie.the rates which are inclusive of all applicable taxes and service charge. Ex: CPAI, MAPAI, APAI.
Allowance	Reversal of charges which were posted before current system/PMS day.
American Plan	A billing arrangement under which room charges include the guestroom and three meals, also known as full board/full pension plan.

Amendment	An amendment is a formal or official change made by the hotel on the request of the guest
Atrium Concept	A design in which the guest rooms overlook the lobby from the first floor to the roof.
Average Occupancy	A ratio that shows rooms sold over a fixed period of time as a percentage of total available rooms in a property of the same period of time.
Average Occupancy Per Room	A ratio that shows the average number of paid guest for each room sold. Calculated by dividing number of paid room guests by number of rooms sold.
Average Room Rate	It is the ratio that is calculated by dividing the room revenue by number of rooms sold. Also known as Average Daily Rate.
Back of the House	Functional areas of the hotel where there is very less or no employee guest interaction.
Balance Sheet	An official financial listing of assets, liabilities and owner's equity.
Banquet Sheet	Listing of details of an event at which food and beverage are served.
Biometrics	An individual electronic measurement of the uniqueness of person such as finger prints and facial gestures.
Blackout	Total loss of electricity.
Block	An agreed upon number of rooms set aside for the members of a group planning to stay in a hotel.
Blocking on horizon	Reserving guest rooms in distant future.
Bottom up	A sales method that involves presenting the least expensive rate first.

Cabana	A guestroom adjacent to the pool area with or without sleeping facilities.
Cancellation	Reservation voided by the guest.
Cancellation Hour	A specific time after which a property may release for sale all unclaimed non-guaranteed reservations according to the property's policy.
Card Key	Plastic card used in place of a metallic key to open a guest room door. These require electronic locks.
Cashier's Report	A daily cash control report that lists cashier activity of cash, credit cards and machine totals by cashier shift.
Casino Hotel	A hotel that features legal gambling with the hotel's operation.
Centre City Hotel	Full service hotel located in the downtown.
Channel Management	It is the objective review of the most profitable marketing approach for guestrooms, CRS, GDS etc.
Check-in	Procedure of guest arrival and registration.
Check-out	Procedure of guest departure and settling down their accounts.
City Ledger Account	A collection of accounts receivable of non-registered guests who use the hotel services.
Commercial Hotel/ Transient hotel	Downtown property that usually caters to the business clients.
Commercial Rates	Room rates for which business people that represent a company but do not necessarily have a bargaining power because of their infrequent pattern of travel.

Complimentary Occupancy Percentage	A ratio that shows the percentage of occupied rooms that are complimentary and generate no revenue.
Complimentary Room	It is an occupied room for which the guest is not charged.
Concierge	An employee whose basic task is to serve as the guest's liaison with hotel and non hotel attraction facilities, services and activities.
Condominium Hotel	A hotel in which an investor takes title to a specific hotel room which remains in the pool to be rented to transient guests whenever the investor is not using the room. Investor expects to receive a gain from the increase in value of the hotel over time as well as receive on going income from rental of his room.
Conducted Tour	A sightseeing program of the destination conducted by a guide that is pre arranged.
Conference Call	A conversation in which three or more people interact over phone.
Confirmed Booking	When reservation is guaranteed with credit card, vouchers etc.
Continental Plan	Room rates does include continental breakfast.
Convention Guest	Guest who attends a large convention and receive a special room rates. These rates depend upon the frequency of booking by the same firm.
Corporate Client	A regular guest who provides business to the hotel and is a part of the corporate that has a tie-up with the hotel.
Corporate Rates	Room rates offered to the corporate clients staying in the hotel.

Credit Balance	The amount of balance the hotel owes guest in the future services.
Credit/House Limit	A limit assigned by the hotel to the guest or company accounts.
Cruise Ship	Ships providing variety of activities and entertainment and can be thought of as floating resort hotels.
Customer Relationship Management	A system that allows hotel managers to integrate technology to support customer service techniques that provide the top notch services.
Cut-off-Date	The date agreed upon by the guest and the hotel after which all unreserved rooms in the block will be released back to general availability.
Daily Blocking	Assigning guests to their particular rooms on a daily basis.
Daily Sales Report	Financial activity report produced by sales department reflecting daily sales activity with cash register tapes or POS audit tapes.
Database interface	Sharing information among computers.
Day Rate	Special room rate for less than an overnight stay.
Debit	Increase in an asset or decrease in the liability.
Debit Balance	Amount of money guest owes the hotel.
Debit Cards	Embossed plastic cards with a magnetic strip on the back side that authorize direct transfer of fund from a customer's bank account to hotel's account for services used.
Deep Cleaning	A thorough cleaning of furniture and accessories, windows etc.

Demographic Data	Size, density, distribution and vital stats of population broken into age, sex, marital status and occupation categories.
Doorknob Menu	A type of room service menu that a housekeeper can leave in the guestroom. It lists a limited number of breakfast items and times of the day that meal can be served, after using this service guest hangs it outside on knob to be collected later and served at that time.
Double	Guestroom assigned to two people.
Double Locked Room	An occupied room in which the guest has turned the main locking knob and which cannot be opened with a key card.
Due Outs	Guests expected to check out on a given day, which have not checked out yet.
Early Arrival	A guest who arrives at hotel before the time of his/her reservation.
Early Makeup	A room status term indicating that the guest has reserved a nearly check-in time or has requested their room to be cleaned as soon as possible.
Electronic Key	Plastic card with code embedded on the magnetic strip.
Escort	A person, usually employed by a tour operator who accompanies a tour from departure to return and serves as a guide.
Escorted Tour	A group of travellers travelling with a guide who has travel experience and has set up an itinerary for the group.
European Plan	Room rates does not include any meals.

Expected Arrival/ Departure Report	A daily report showing number and names of guests expected to arrive in reservations as well as the number and names of guests expected to depart.
Expected Departure List	A daily report showing number of guests expected to depart, number of stay over and the name of guests associated with each transaction.
Express Check-out	Means by which the guest uses computer technology in the guest room or a computer in the hotel lobby to check-out.
Familiarization (FAM) Tour	A reduced rate/complimentary tour offered to travel agents, whole sellers, incentive travel planners, travel writers to promote a hotel or destinations.
Family Rate	A special room rate for parents and children occupying one guest room.
Float	The delay in the payment from an account after using a credit card.
Floor Limit	A dollar amount set by the credit card agency that allows for a maximum amount of guest charges.
Folio	The guest's bill that all hotel and incidental charges are posted to.
Foreign Independent Traveller	A tour created for individuals/families who walk in a travel agency and tell them what country they want to visit.
Front Desk	The focal point of activity within the hotel usually prominently located in the hotel lobby. Guests are registered, assigned rooms and checked out at the front desk.

Front Desk Agent	Hotel employee whose responsibilities centre on the registration process but also include pre-registration activities, room status co-ordination and mail, message and information requests.
Front of the House	The functional areas of the hotel in which employees have extensive guest contact such as front desk and dining rooms.
Front Office	Hotel's department responsible for processing reservations, registering guests, settling guest accounts and checking guests in and out.
Full Service Hotel	A hotel with a full range of services and amenities which may include some or all; on site restaurant and lounge, meeting facility, pool, fitness centre etc.
General Ledger	Collection of accounts that the controller uses to organize the financial activities of hotel.
Global Distribution System	A distribution channel for reservations that provide worldwide distribution of hotel reservation information and allows selling hotel reservations around the world usually accomplished by connecting the hotel reservation system with an airline reservation system. Ex: Amadeus, Saber etc.
Group Pick Up	The guestrooms that are actually rented by a group that are held in a group reservation.
Group Rates	Room rate offered to large groups of people visiting the hotel for a common reason.

Group Reservation	A block of multiple rooms that are being held under an individual name at a particular hotel for a specific date or range of dates. Generally used for conventions, meetings, receptions, weddings etc.
Group Travellers	People who are travelling on business or for pleasure in an organized fashion.
Guaranteed Reservations	A reservation that is guaranteed by the guest to be paid even in the case of a no show.
Guest Comment Card	Short questionnaires that lodging and food service establishments ask their guests to fill out. Guest comments are used by rhe property to define current markets and improve the operations.
Guest Cycle	Division of the flow of business though a hotel that identifies the physical contacts and financial exchanges between the guest and the hotel.
Guest Folio	A form imprinted with hotel's logo and control number and has space for room number, guest identification, data in and data out, and room rate in the upper left corner. It allows for guest charges to be imprinted with PMS and is filled in room number sequence.
Guest History Card	A record of guest's visits including rooms as assigned rates, special needs and credit ratings.
Guest Information Services	Automated information devices in public hotel areas that enable guest to obtain information about in house events and local activities.

Guest Profile	A list of the characteristics that property's guest have in common. The guest profile helps management to identify which market segment the property appeals to and which segment the property wants to attract.
Guest Relations	The establishment of personal rapport and goodwill with guests through service and attention to individual guest needs.
Guest Supplies	Also known as guest amenities such as small bottles of shampoo, lotion etc.
Guestroom Control Book	A book used to monitor the number of guestrooms committed to a group, controlling guestroom booking activity providing the sales office the max. number of rooms it can sell to the group in a given day.
Guestroom Key	A key that opens a single guestroom if it is not double locked.
Guestroom Maintenance	A form of preventive maintenance involving inspection of number of items in guestroom when needed .
Hospitality Industry	Food and lodging service business that provide short term services against money.
Hospitality Suite	A room used for entertainment.
Hotel	A hotel is a commercial establishment that provides decent and up-scale services in food and shelter to the guest against money.
Hotel Chain	A group of affiliated hotels.

Hotel Guest Cycle	The sequence of phases that begin with pre-scale events, continues through POS activities and concludes with post-sales transaction. The phases identify the physical contact and financial exchange that occur between guest and various centres within the hotel.
Hotel Management Company	A company that is hired to professionally manage a hotel for other owners.
Hotel Representative	An individual who offers hotel reservations to whole sellers, travel agents & the public. He may be paid by the hotel they represent on a fee basis or by commission.
House Count	Number of people registered into a hotel on a specific night.
House Limit	A guest credit limit predetermined by management officials.
Housekeeping Department	A department responsible for cleaning the hotel guestrooms and public areas.
Housekeeping Room Status	Terminology that indicates availability of guest room such as available, clean, occupied, dirty, stay over, on change, and out of order.
Hubbart Formula	Method used to compute room rate that considers factors like operating expenses, desired returns on investment and income from various departments in the hotel.
IDS	Internet Distribution System.
Imprest Money	An **imprest** is a **cash** amount which is given to the cashier to pay for small & routine expenses. it is replenished routinely to maintain that balance
Inbound Tourist	Tourist entering a particular country

Incentive Travels	Travels financed by a business as an employee incentive.
Inclusive Tour	A tour in which all the elements(air fare, hotels, etc) are included for a flat rate. An inclusive tour rate does not necessarily cover all costs.
Independent Food Service Operation	An operation owned by an owner/ owners with one or more properties having no chain relationship. Menus, food purchase specifications, operating procedures etc may differ among owned properties.
Independent Hotels	A hotel with no chain/franchise affiliation. It may be owned by an individual proprietor or a group of investors.
In-house Laundry	A hotel operated department that launders linens, uniforms etc.
Inn	A smaller lodging facility with limited services and one to three stories.
In-room guest console	A multi feature phone that may include functions like alarm, radio, remote control of heating, ventilation and air conditioner, television and room lights etc.
Inter-departmental Communications	Communications between departments.
Interfacing	The ability of computer to communicate electronically and share data.
International Tourism	Travel people make outside their residing country.
Itinerary	A plan of Journey
Job Analysis	A detailed listing of task performed in a job, which provides the basis for a sound job description.

Job Description	A listing of required duties to be performed by an employee in a particular job.
Lanai	A guestroom with a balcony or patio overlooking water body.
Landmark	Distinguishing feature that stands out & provides a reference point for orientation. They also provide travellers with information about directions and distances.
Late Arrival	A guest holding a reservation who plans to arrive after the property's designated cancellation hour and so notify's the property.
Late Charge	A transaction requiring posting to a guest account that does not reach the front office for posting before the guest had checked out or done the final settlement.
Late Check-out	A guest who is being allowed to check-out later than the property's standard check-out times.
Leisure Travellers	People who travel alone or with others on their own for visits to points of interest, to relatives or for other personal reasons.
Liabilities	Financial or other contractual obligations or debts.
Limited Services	A level of service provided by a hotel with guestroom accommodations and limited food services and meeting space.
Lodge	A lodging facility that is generally small and are located in rustic outdoors of the city.

Log Book	Located at reception containing instructions/information/happenings/handover of the day to know of.
Long Stay	A guest who stays for more than certain number of days.
Long Term Stay/ Relocation Guest	Those individuals relocating to an area who require lodging until permanent housing is found.
Luxury Hotel	A hotel with high room rates that features exceptional service and amenities.
Manager's Report	A listing of occupancy stats from previous day, viz occupancy percentage, yield percentage, average daily reate, rev PAR and number of guests.
Market Segment	Identifiable group of customers with similar needs for products and services.
Marquee	The curbside message board which includes the logo of the hotel and space for a message.
Mass Marketing	Advertising products and services through mass communication modes.
Mass Tourism	Wide scale travel by a large number of people brought about by the increase in leisure time, reliable and in-expensive modes of transportation .
Master Folio	A bill that has all charges for the members of a group are posted in.
Master Key	A key that can open all the guest rooms that are not double locked.
Material Safety Data Sheet(MSDS)	A listing of chemical contents relative hazards to the users and name and address of the producers of content.

Mid-price/Extended stay hotels	Hotel that caters mostly to people who must be in an area for a week or more. The rooms have more living space and less expensive as compared to regular hotels.
Modified American Plan	A room rate offers one meal with the price of a room rental.
Motel	A smaller lodging facility with limited services and one to two stories with exterior entrance rooms that guests can drive up to.
National Tourism Office	Primary government agency responsible for implementing national goals and public policy with respect to tourism and for providing information services to international travellers.
No Show	A guest who made a reservation but did not check in.
NO-Post	Special functionality of the PMS to activate the NO POST on reservations. This will stop any extra charges from other outlets or connected systems to be charged to guest room.
Occupancy Report	A report prepared each night by a front desk agent that lists rooms occupied that night and also the lists those guests expected to checkout the following day.
Occupied	A room status term indicating that a guest is currently registered to the room.
Online Reservation System	An internet based system used by the hotels that allow prospective hotel guest to check availability and make reservation at the hotel.
OTA	Online Travel Agents.

Out Bound Tourist	Tourist travelling abroad for business or leisure.
Overbooking	Accepting more reservations than actual rooms.
Overstay	A guest who remains at the property after his stated departure date.
Package	A special offering of products & services created by a hotel to increase sales. It includes guestroom, meals and the use of property's recreational facilities at special rates.
Package Tour	Tour put together by a tour operator that offers at all inclusive price, several travel elements which a traveller would otherwise purchase separately.
Point -of-Sale	Computerized systems that retail outlets such as restaurants etc. enter orders and maintain various accounting information. It generally interfaces with the PMS.
Policy and Procedure Manual	Publication that provides an outline of how the specific duties of each job are to be performed.
Potential Gross Income	The amount of sales a hotel might obtain at a given level of occupancy, average daily rate and anticipated yield.
Pre-authorization	We block certain amount in/from the guest account using credit card details and further transactions are made from that blocked amount only.
Profit and Loss Statement	A listing of revenues and expenses for a certain time period.

Property Booking Engine	An internet reservation system that is owned and operated by an individual hotel or group to allow them to take reservation on their own website without paying a fee to GDS, third party booking engines etc.
Property Management System	PMS is a computerized front desk system that manages hotel room inventory, guest billing, and interfaces with various other systems.
Quad	A guestroom with occupancy of four pax.
Queen	Bed size approximately (60X80) inches.
Rack Rate	The current rate charged for each accommodation as established by property's management.
Registration Card	A form on which the guest indicates the name, home or billing address, phone number, date of departure, etc.
Retention	It is charged for a reservation if a guaranteed reservation has been cancelled or had become no show
Reservation	A room being held under an individual or business's name at a particular hotel for specific date or range of dates.
Reservation Agent	An employee either in FO or in a separate department who is responsible for all aspects of reservation processing.
Reservation department	A department within a hotel's room division staffed by skilled telemarketing personnel who takes reservations of guests and answers queries efficiently.
Reservation Status	An indicator of the room's long term availability for assignment.

Residential Hotel	Hotels that provide long term accommodation to the guest.
Resort Hotel	A hotel located at a desirable vacation spot that offers fine dining & exceptional services that are unavailable at most of the properties.
Revenue Management	A process of planning to achieve maximum room rate and most profitable guests that encourages front office manager, general manager and marketing /sales director to target sales period and to develop sales program that will maximize profit for the hotel.
Room Allotment Report	A report that summarizes the rooms committed by future date.
Room Data Card	A card used to record information concerning the basic characteristics and major elements of an individual guest room.
Room Division	The largest and usually most profitable division in the hotel. It has four departments: Front office, Reservations, Housekeeping & uniformed services.
Room Occupancy Sensor	A device that uses infrared lights and ultrasonic sound waves to sense the physical occupancy of the room. It can turn on & off the devices when person enters or leaves room.
Room Rate	The price a hotel charges for overnight accommodations.
Room Revenue	The amount of revenue received through room sales.

Room Sales Projections	A weekly report prepared and distributed by the front office manager that indicates the number of arrivals, departures, walk-ins, stayovers and no-shows.
Room Status	Information about the current and future availability of room in a hotel. Current availability is determined through H/K data and future's is done by reservation data.
Room Status Discrepancy	A situation in which the H/K department's description of room's status differs from the room status information that guides FO staff In assigning the rooms.
Room Status Report	A report that indicates the current status of rooms according to the H/K designations such as: on-makeup, on-charge, out-of-order, clean & inspection ready.
Rooms Checklist	A list, used for guest room maintenance, of all the items in the guest room with a brief notation opposite each item of the type of inspection activities to be performed.
Sale Indicators	Number of guests and revenue generated.
Scanty Baggage	A guest who checks-in to the hotel with very less or no luggage
Self Check-in Process	A procedure that requires the guest to insert a credit card into a self check-in terminal and answer a few simple questions concerning the guest's stay.
Service Charge	Percentage of the bill(10%-20%) added to guest's charge for distribution to service employees in lieu of direct tipping.

Series Group	Group in this category arrive in series and follow the same itinerary one after another for a specific period of time, say one year
Single bed	Bed size approximately (36X75) inches.
Skipper	A guest who leaves with no intentions of paying for the room.
Stay over	A room status term indicating that the guest is not checking out & will stay for at least one more night.
Studio	A guest room having one or two sofa-cum-beds.
Suite hotel	A hotel whose sleeping rooms have separate bedrooms and lining room or parlor areas and perhaps kitchenettes.
TA	Travel agent who receives commission for booking.
Tentative Booking	When reservation is waiting booker's confirmation.
Tour	Any pre-arranged journey to one or more places and back to the point of origins.
Tour Operator	A business that puts travel tours & sells them directly to individuals or by travel agencies.
Transient Hotel	Hotels which cater to business people and tend to busiest from Mondays to Thursdays.
Twin Rooms	A guest room with two twin beds.
Under stay	A guest who checks out before his stated departure.
Up selling	A sales technique where a guest is offered a more expensive room then what they reserved actually & then persuaded to rent the room based on room's features.

Upgrade	To move to a better accommodation or class of service.
Vacant	Room status term indicating that the room has been cleaned and inspected and is ready for the arriving guest.
Void	Reversal of charges which were posted on same day.
Valet parking	Is a service that operates at places such as hotels & restaurants, in which guest car are parked by an attendant
VISA	Visitors International Stay Admission
Waitlisted booking	Reservation kept on hold due to hotel being overbooked.
Walk-in guest	A guest who arrives at the hotel without prior reservations.

Common Abbreviations used in the Front Office Department

CP	Continental Plan
EP	European Plan
MAP	Modified American Plan
AP	American Plan
HLP	Heat light power
FIT	Free individual traveller
GIT	Group inclusive traveller/tour
DFIT	Domestic free individual traveller
FFIT	Foreign free individual traveller
CVGR	Corporate volume guaranteed rate
MICE	Meeting incentive conference events
OPERA	Open process engine for reliable activities
OTA	Online travel agent
OOO	Out of order

OS	Out of service
IS	Inspected
RSVP	Respondez, s'ilvous plait
CIP	Commercially important person
BAR	Best available rate
DND	Do not disturb
NEFT	National electronic fund transfer
RTGS	Real-time gross settlement
IMT	Instant money transfer
BTC	Bill to company
FHRAI	Federation of hotels & restaurants association of India
HRANI	Hotel and restaurants association of north India
GDS	Global distribution system
CRS	Central reservation system
POS	Point of sale
RSO	Regional sales office
EDC	Electronic data capturing
EA	Expected arrival
ED	Expected departure
AI	All inclusive
GR	Guest registration
RLM	Restricted license money
FRRO	Foreigner regional registration office
PSU	Presidential suite
IC room	Interconnecting room
DL	Double lock
DO	Due out
ARR	Average room revenue/rate

REVPAR	Revenue per available room
OCC	Occupancy
CUG	Closed user group
MICR	Magnetic ink character recognition
VAT	Value added tax
GST	Goods and service tax
GSTS	Guest satisfaction tracking system
FTO	Foreign tour operator
TA	Travel agent
TDS	Tax Deduction at source
DSR	Daily sales report
LEED	Leadership in energy and environmental design
TCMS	Tea coffee milk and sugar
VPO	Visitor paid out
DB	Double bed
TWB	Twin bed
LLR	Left luggage room
ED	early departure
MTD	Month to date
YTD	Year to date
RCI	Resort condominiums international

D. Generic Interview Questions

Q1. Introduce yourself / tell me about yourself?

Q2. Why do you want to join our organization?

Q3. What preparation you have done to appear in this interview?

Q4. What are you strength & weakness?

Q5. What are your hobbies beside the work?

Q6. Why should we hire you/ why do you think you are perfect for this position?

Q7. What do you know about the company?

Q8. Where do you see yourself five years from now?

Q9. What are your career goals in the hotel industry?

Q10. If you get this job, how long do you see yourself staying with us?

Q11. As job is repetitive, How would you encourage yourself to work well regularly?

Q12 Tell us your ability to work under pressure and how much stress you can handle?

Q13. How would you feel about working in night shift?

Q14. What does excellent guest service mean to you?

Q15. How will you convince an unsatisfied guest of our hotel?

Q16. Why are you leaving your current job?

Q17. Share the experience about you old company?

Q18. Tell me a challenge of conflict you have faced at work and how you have handled it?

Q19. What is your salary expectation?

Q20. Do you have any questions for us?